THE BEATLES

Other titles in the
People Who Made History series:

PEOPLE WHO MADE HISTORY

THE BEATLES

David M. Haugen, *Book Editor*

Bruce Glassman, *Vice President*
Bonnie Szumski, *Publisher*
Helen Cothran, *Managing Editor*

GREENHAVEN PRESS
An imprint of Thomson Gale, a part of The Thomson Corporation

THOMSON

GALE

Detroit • New York • San Francisco • San Diego • New Haven, Conn.
Waterville, Maine • London • Munich

LIBRARY OF CONGRESS CATALOGING-IN-PUBLICATION DATA

The Beatles / David M. Haugen, book editor.
  p. cm. — (People who made history)
  Includes bibliographical references and index.
  ISBN 0-7377-2595-8 (lib. : alk. paper)
    1. Beatles. 2. Rock musicians—England—Biography. I. Haugen, David M.,
  1969– . II. Series.
  ML421.B4H46 2005
  782.42166'092'2—dc22   2004040596
  [B]

CONTENTS

Chapter 3: Experiments

Chapter 4: Disunion

Chapter 5: Legacy

FOREWORD

In the vast and colorful pageant of human history, a handful of individuals stand out. They are the men and women who have come variously to be called "great," "leading," "brilliant," "pivotal," or "infamous" because they and their deeds forever changed their own society or the world as a whole. Some were political or military leaders—kings, queens, presidents, generals, and the like—whose policies, conquests, or innovations reshaped the maps and futures of countries and entire continents. Among those falling into this category were the formidable Roman statesman/general Julius Caesar, who extended Rome's power into Gaul (what is now France); Caesar's lover and ally, the notorious Egyptian queen Cleopatra, who challenged the strongest male rulers of her day; and England's stalwart Queen Elizabeth I, whose defeat of the mighty Spanish Armada saved England from subjugation.

Some of history's other movers and shakers were scientists or other thinkers whose ideas and discoveries altered the way people conduct their everyday lives or view themselves and their place in nature. The electric light and other remarkable inventions of Thomas Edison, for example, revolutionized almost every aspect of home-life and the workplace; and the theories of naturalist Charles Darwin lit the way for biologists and other scientists in their ongoing efforts to understand the origins of living things, including human beings.

Still other people who made history were religious leaders and social reformers. The struggles of the Arabic prophet Muhammad more than a thousand years ago led to the establishment of one of the world's great religions—Islam; and the efforts and personal sacrifices of an American reverend named Martin Luther King Jr. brought about major improvements in race relations and the justice system in the United States.

Each anthology in the People Who Made History series begins with an introductory essay that provides a general overview of the individual's life, times, and contributions. The group of essays that follow are chosen for their accessibility to a young adult audience and carefully edited in consideration of the reading and comprehension levels of that audience. Some of the essays are by noted historians, professors, and other experts. Others are excerpts from contemporary writings by or about the pivotal individual in question. To aid the reader in choosing the material of immediate interest or need, an annotated table of contents summarizes the article's main themes and insights.

Each volume also contains extensive research tools, including a collection of excerpts from primary source documents pertaining to the individual under discussion. The volumes are rounded out with an extensive bibliography and a comprehensive index.

Plutarch, the renowned first-century Greek biographer and moralist, crystallized the idea behind Greenhaven's People Who Made History when he said, "To be ignorant of the lives of the most celebrated men of past ages is to continue in a state of childhood all our days." Indeed, since it is people who make history, every modern nation, organization, institution, invention, artifact, and idea is the result of the diligent efforts of one or more individuals, living or dead; and it is therefore impossible to understand how the world we live in came to be without examining the contributions of these individuals.

INTRODUCTION: THE MAKING AND UNMAKING OF THE BEATLES

In late 2003, Apple Corps released the latest Beatles' album, *Let It Be . . . Naked.* This was not a new record by Liverpool's Fab Four but a reengineered version of their *Let It Be* album that, although recorded in January 1969, was released in May 1970—after the band's demise. The delay of the album's original release was due to the band's continual dissatisfaction with the recordings and the individual Beatles' personal squabbles. In March 1970, fed up with the project and each other, the Beatles dropped the album in the hands of legendary producer Phil Spector, who was given carte blanche to remix the album as he saw fit. Spector, famed for his "wall of sound" technique that gave simple pop songs an often-overblown symphonic dimension, left his trademark touch on several of the album's tracks. *Let It Be* received the 2003 overhaul to strip away much of the remixing and over-dubbed instrumentation that Spector had added to the Beatles' songs. According to Paul McCartney, one of the two surviving Beatles in late 2003, *Let It Be . . . Naked* was an attempt to show the world that even in 1969—amidst the bickering and internal decay that *Let It Be* came to symbolize—the Beatles were "a good little band."[1]

NEVER A "LITTLE BAND"

McCartney's comment is certainly disingenuous. In their time, John Lennon, Paul McCartney, George Harrison, and Ringo Starr comprised the preeminent pop group in the world—and to many Beatles fans today, they still are. In their brief career, the Beatles had racked up twenty number-one singles in the U.S. *Billboard* chart, and fifteen of their albums also reached number one in America. The main songwriting force of Lennon and McCartney produced a bible of well-crafted pop songs that have become a staple for classic rock listeners as well as templates for successive generations of singers and musicians. But the Beatles' influence upon the world did not rest merely upon their music; the band combined youthful charm, quick wit, and novel appearance with their talent, and marketers skillfully foisted the whole package upon eager fans. The resulting Beatlemania of the mid-1960s was a cultural phenomenon of unparalleled scope. As biographer and fan Nicholas Schaffner writes, the Beatles "seemed to transform . . . the look, sound, and style of at least one generation. They had, of course, a lot of help from a great many friends—but it was more than anyone else, John, Paul, George, and Ringo who set in motion the forces that made a whole era what it was, and, by extension, what it is today."[2] As Schaffner suggests, the Beatles and Beatlemania helped define the decade of the 1960s. And like the Vietnam War, the youth counterculture, and other touchstones of that era, the whole Beatles phenomenon continued to influence future generations in profound ways.

What, then, are modern readers to make of Paul McCartney's deceptively humble comment about *Let It Be . . . Naked?* The key lies in understanding the turmoil and bad blood that characterized the collapse of the Fab Four. McCartney then, as now, knew the Beatles could not last. By 1969 it was clear that the band members were growing apart—friendships were strained, musical interests were diverging, and the glow of Beatlemania had (thankfully to the Beatles) faded. Even though the Beatles put together another album of music after the recording sessions for *Let It Be*, it was *Let It Be* that manifested the problems that would break the band apart even before the record was released. McCartney's current appraisal acknowledges that sense of foreboding. Despite the gathering gloom of 1969, the songs on *Let It Be* still reveal a band with the power to create good, lasting music. What is perhaps more interesting about the comment, however, is that it is an attempt to reduce the Beatles to just another rock-and-roll band. McCartney's self-deprecation and humility ring hollow, though. The Beatles of 1969 could never again be the Beatles who played the tiny Cavern Club in 1961 or 1962 (when Ringo Starr joined the band). But there is a sense of nostalgia in McCartney's words, as if he—or perhaps the world—could strip away the corrosive elements responsible for the band's demise in 1970 and remember the Beatles as merely another talented quartet from the early 1960s Liverpool scene. That, of course, could also never happen. For as McCartney himself must have realized, the same elements that went into making the world's greatest pop band were the same elements—transformed over time—that unmade the Beatles as well.

FRIENDS AND MUSICIANS

Friendship and a love of music were the two primary elements that brought the members of the Beatles together. Although the band's final lineup of John, Paul, George, and Ringo would not be cemented until 1962, the core friendships began several years before. John Lennon and Paul McCartney met in July 1957 when Lennon's on-again-off-again band, the Quarry Men, played a church social in their hometown of Liverpool, England. Like many other aspiring youth in England; sixteen-year-old Lennon was a guitar player trying his hand at imitating the Elvis Presley rock-and-roll sound coming out of the United States and the jug band–like skiffle sound made popular in England by Lonnie Donegan. Fifteen-year-old McCartney was also taken with the skiffle craze as well as with Elvis, Bill Haley, and other American rock pioneers. Realizing their similar musical tastes and their love of guitar, Lennon and McCartney hit it off, and in October of that year, McCartney officially joined the Quarry Men. Soon after, McCartney started writing original songs for the Quarry Men, and Lennon, not wishing to be shown up in his own band, penned a few of his own tunes. The friendly rivalry turned to collaboration that would eventually produce some of the most memorable songs of the next decade.

The friendship that began in October 1957 blossomed immediately. As biographer Hunter Davies writes, "What happened in the subsequent months was that John and Paul got to know each other. They spent all their time together. They both stayed away from school and went to Paul's house, while his dad was out at work, and ate fried eggs and practiced guitar chords."[5] The pair became infatuated with being musicians. Unfortunately, other members of the Quarry Men did not feel that dedication, and several friends passed through the ranks in the band's formative years. In 1959, however, the core duo became a trio when fourteen-year-old George Harrison, a schoolmate of McCartney's, joined. Harrison was already versed in guitar basics when he became a Quarry Man, but he was comparatively young. His age initially deterred Lennon from allowing Harrison to join up, but Harrison's guitar playing was the deciding factor—he simply knew more chords that Lennon or McCartney. And, over time, it was obvious that Harrison was the best guitar player of the three. The trio—with a stand-in drummer—would play any public venue that they could, but most of their time was spent at school or practicing in Harrison's or McCartney's houses. The days together cemented their friendship and their devotion to the group.

THE OTHER BEATLES

In January 1960, the guitar-heavy Quarry Men added a much-needed bass player. Stuart Sutcliffe was a friend of Lennon's from art school. Though a talented visual artist, Sutcliffe had no strong musical skill. He was persuaded by Lennon to devote some of his money, earned through the sale of one of his paintings, to buy a bass and join the band. According to Beatles' biographer Gareth L. Pawlowski, "Stu eventually learned a few chords but his contribution as a musician was nil."[4] Still, Sutcliffe was a fast friend of Lennon's, and he stuck with the band through its first two tours of Germany. The other new member of the group to sign on before the first German tour was drummer Pete Best. An acquaintance of Harrison's, Best was the son of a small-time Liverpool club owner. He was drafted into the band by necessity, not necessarily through friendship. The Quarry Men—who had been rechristened "the Beatals" by Sutcliffe and then "the Silver Beatles" by fellow musician Brian Cassar—had been offered a deal to play several gigs in Hamburg, Germany, if they had a complete band. Not willing to pass up the opportunity, the group enlisted Best and headed for the bright lights of the Reeperbahn.

In Hamburg, the quintet, booked simply as "the Beatles," developed into a close-knit unit. They lived in tight quarters, sleeping—when they could—in a cellar beneath a nearby cinema. Being foreigners, they primarily relied on each other for amusement. Most of their time, however, was spent working hard, spending up to twelve hours a day onstage. Through these demanding shows, the boys engendered a presence and a collective personality. They adopted a single look, dressing in leather outfits and slicking their hair back like the rebel rockers of the time. With a club audience that didn't speak English, the group simply learned to play loud and fast. According to Lennon, "It was Hamburg. That's where we really developed. To get the Germans going and keep it up for twelve hours at a time, we really had to hammer. We'd try anything we could think of because there was nobody to copy. So we played what we liked and the Germans liked it, too, as long as it was loud."[5] And when volume didn't stir the crowd, the Beatles indulged in crazy antics—telling jokes, insulting the patrons, and hurling themselves into each other in raucous displays on stage.

The unity of the band while on the first tour of Hamburg was fairly sound, but some element of division began to creep in as the continual performances and the hours spent together took their toll. Nerves naturally frayed. As Hunter Davies records, "The Beatles had lots of arguments among themselves, but nothing serious. It was mainly Stu and Pete, the relatively new boys, being picked on by the rest. Stu took it to heart, but Pete didn't seem to notice."[6] Sutcliffe perhaps got most of the ribbing because he had fallen in love with a twenty-two-year-old photographer's assistant named Astrid Kirchherr. She was instrumental in introducing the Beatles to the art crowd in Hamburg, and she took a personal interest in the band—especially in Sutcliffe. At the end of the first tour of Hamburg in 1960, Sutcliffe declined to return to the Liverpool scene with his band mates, choosing instead to reenroll in art school in Hamburg and share his life with Kirchherr.

The four remaining Beatles soldiered on, with Paul now taking up the bass guitar. United, they made the most of what they had learned in Germany. The loud, fast playing, coupled with stage antics, began earning them a reputation in their hometown. They set up camp in the Cavern Club in early 1961 and played to packed houses. But almost as quickly as they had put down stakes, they were booked on a second tour of Germany. Sutcliffe played a few dates with the band when the band arrived back in Hamburg, but it was evident that his future lay with his studies. When the Beatles returned to Liverpool in July, they again took up residence in the Cavern Club. It was there, in November 1961, that the second contributing factor of the Beatles' rise to fame would walk in and attend a lunchtime session.

A MANAGER

Brian Epstein was a manager in his father's NEMS music store in Liverpool. According to Epstein's autobiography, a young man had come into his store on October 28 looking for a single that featured the Beatles. The record, "My Bonnie," on which the Beatles played in support of singer Tony Sheridan, had been recorded in Germany during their last tour. Only a few copies had reached England, but the sudden popularity of the band at the Cavern Club had sent new fans in search of the elusive disc. Epstein had not heard of the group, but he became intrigued when subsequent visitors inquired about the same single. He decided to take in a lunchtime show at the Cavern Club on November 9.

In his autobiography, Epstein recalled his initial reaction to the Beatles:

> They were not very tidy and not very clean. But they were tidier and cleaner than anyone else who performed at that lunchtime session or, for that matter, at most of the sessions I later attended. I had never seen anything like the Beatles on any stage. They smoked as they played and they ate and talked and pretended to hit each other. They turned their backs on the audience and shouted at them and laughed at private jokes.[7]

"But," Epstein continued, "they gave a captivating and honest show and they had very considerable magnetism. I loved their ad libs and I was fascinated by this, to me, new music with its pounding bass beat and its vast engulfing sound."[8] Epstein was so taken, in fact, that he asked the Beatles to stop by the NEMS store in December "just for a chat." Over the course of a few chats in December, Brian Epstein offered to manage the band. For a quarter of their earnings, Epstein promised to get the band better pay, gigs outside of Liverpool, and a record contract with a major label. Speaking for himself and his three mates, John Lennon accepted immediately. Now it was up to Epstein—who had no experience managing a band—to make good on his promises.

EPSTEIN'S INFLUENCE

Epstein's influence on the Beatles was immeasurable. As he began making local connections to get better-paying gigs, he had his eyes set on securing a major label deal. To make the band more marketable in this respect, he completely retooled the Beatles image. The leather outfits were replaced by smart, matching suits, and the stage antics were toned down. As Pete Best recalled, "He claimed that no one in the world of entertainment outside our present environment would tolerate our slovenly look, our chatting to the birds near the stage, our eating and drinking on the stand, our playful butting and jostling and generally enjoying ourselves. Discipline was what we needed most." Best admits that there was some protest—especially from John Lennon, "but in the end we all conformed."[9] The band recognized that their own efforts had not gotten them very far after their Hamburg tours, so they were willing to trust in Epstein. And in January 1962, the trust seemed to pay off when Epstein announced that he had secured for them a studio recording session with Decca Records—in hopes of attaining a contract.

Nineteen sixty-two, indeed, showed great promise for the Beatles. While the group waited to hear about the results of the January audition, their daily lives as performers had noticeably improved under Epstein's management. As biographer Mark Lewisohn summarizes:

> By the end of January . . . the Beatles had a decent and fair management contract, a record in the shops, a possible contract with the mighty Decca organization in the offing, an audition with BBC radio lined up for 12 February, a much superior Hamburg engagement to fulfill in the spring, money in their pockets, and a rota of new and vastly-improved venues to play. Out went the great majority of the Beatles' 1961 live venues, deemed unsuitable by Epstein for his group, out went the Beatles' uncaring attitude, their childish stage antics and reputation for poor punctuality. And out, too, went the group's hit-and-miss music presentation, to be replaced by one or two precise, pre-arranged sets of never more than 60 minutes.[10]

By February, the new regimen was a welcome relief to the old system of touring, but news of the possible record deal from Decca was not favorable. The executives decided against signing the band. Though dispirited, Epstein took the session tapes and continued to shop them around. Within the first weeks of the month, they ended up in the hands of EMI representatives who passed them along to artists and repertoire chief George Martin at Parlophone Records, an EMI label.

GOOD NEWS, BAD NEWS

For three months, Epstein and the Beatles waited for word from Martin. They continued performing, and the band even made a third trip to Hamburg in April. Sadly, on this visit, they learned that their old friend and band mate, Stu Sutcliffe, had died of a brain hemorrhage. The news was grievous, but on its heels followed a May telegram from Epstein saying that George Martin had offered the band a chance to record for Parlophone. On June 6, four days after returning from Germany, the Beatles were in EMI's Abbey Road studios for the first time. But as with the Decca audition, no contract had been offered, so only time would tell if Epstein would finally make good on his promise.

According to Brian Epstein, the recording for Parlophone went well. George Martin liked what he heard—at least most of it anyway. As Epstein recalled, "George Martin had not been too happy about Pete Best's drumming."[11] Apparently he was not the only one. According to Mark Lewisohn:

> The Beatles had been contemplating the dismissal of Pete Best for some considerable time and, in their own deliberate way, were gradually divorcing him from their activities. . . . A plan was hatching in the minds of John, Paul, and George to oust him—it was based largely on jealousy of his good looks and the way he attracted the most girls, but it also went deeper than this. His drumming ability, though adequate, was quite limited and was almost certainly unsuitable for recording purposes, a point which George Martin made quite clear to Brian Epstein on 6 June.[12]

Epstein was given the task of informing Best that he was out of the band. On August 16, he called Best into his office and delivered the news quickly: "The boys want you out and Ringo in."[13] It was an unexpected blow to Best. For two years, he had not heard a complaint against his drumming. And he felt he was equal if not superior to Ringo Starr, the drummer for Rory Storm and the Hurricanes—the man who was to be his replacement. Best was perhaps more disturbed that his bandmates had not had the courage to face him with the news. He also did not know that the Beatles had just been offered a recording contract from Parlophone in July. Best left the band disgruntled and bitter but with no recourse. Two days later, Ringo Starr joined the band, and the Fab Four lineup was ready to change the face of popular music.

THE FAB FOUR

Ringo Starr had met his new bandmates in Hamburg when the Hurricanes had shared the same venue with the Beatles. He hung around with the Beatles in between shows, and they became fast friends. According to George Harrison, the slow divorce from Pete Best and the affinity for Starr happened back then. "When we finished doing [a] gig, Pete would go off on his own and we three would hang out together, and then when Ringo was around it was like a full unit, both on and off stage."[14] Starr was the oldest of the Beatles but only topping Lennon by three months, so he fit right in with the group. He was also a dedicated musician who was eager to devote his energies to making the band a success. And that devotion paid off rather quickly.

The Beatles' stellar rise began soon after George Martin had them return to the studio in September 1962 to record a debut single. When "Love Me Do" was released the following month, it slowly climbed the charts in Britain. After the band fulfilled some previously booked tour dates in Hamburg and Scotland, the Beatles' second single, "Please Please Me," hit in January 1963. "Please Please Me" had a more meteoric climb in the British charts and, thanks to heavy airplay and record company promotion, the record received recognition outside Liverpool. A record album with the same name followed quickly in March. Epstein was then able to garner television appearances and gigs across the country. And instead of playing second to other acts on the bill, the Beatles became the headliners of the shows. The schedule that Epstein set was grueling, but it was paying off. The televised appearances, the numerous stage performances, and the coverage by local press contributed to a growing fan hysteria for the Beatles. Mark Lewisohn acknowledges, "Why the mayhem started, and why it was necessary to those causing it, will forever remain a mystery,"[15] but by late spring of 1963, a phenomenon called "Beatlemania" was spreading throughout England.

BEATLEMANIA

Although interest in the band was swelling in May and June 1963, it wasn't until the Beatles played the London Palladium on October 13, 1963, that the hallmarks of Beatlemania would be set. As friend and biographer Hunter Davies relates:

> Argyll Street, where the Palladium is situated . . . was besieged by fans all day long. Newspapermen started arriving once the stories of the crowds got round. The stage door was blocked by fans, mountains of presents, and piles of telegrams. Inside it was almost impossible to rehearse for the continual screams of the thousands of fans chanting outside in the streets.[16]

The Palladium show was televised and broadcast to millions across England, as were the scenes of crowd hysteria both inside and outside the theater. And these sights were repeated at subsequent gigs at other smaller venues. As Davies writes, "In Britain each one-night stand resulted in the same hysterical crowd scenes. Everyday the newspaper had almost word-for-word the same front-page news stories, only the name of the town was different."[17]

Beatlemania was, of course, not a spontaneous, unplanned event. The outpouring of emotion and the incredible furor of the fans was most likely unexpected—at least to the degree achieved, but Beatlemania did have a science. The weight of the record company's promotional tools was behind the band, making sure there was press coverage and advance notice of shows. Brian Epstein had relentlessly pursued gigs for the group and made the Beatles stick to the tour schedule even as the hysteria grew. And once the momentum caught on, Epstein wisely put the Beatles in front of the camera or a herd of newspaper reporters at every opportunity. By the end of 1963, it was likely that no one in England could claim that he or she had not at least heard of the Beatles.

TAKING ON THE WORLD TOGETHER

For the Beatles themselves, the early days of Beatlemania were a dream come true. Ringo Starr has acknowledged that, to him, success was achieved when the Beatles played the Palladium, since that was where the preeminent bands had always played. Everything after that was more than a Liverpool quartet could hope for. Success for the Beatles, however, continued to mount, but it did not seem to spoil the band members. They had few opportunities to indulge in their fame. The tour schedule, which lasted into the following year, left the Fab Four with little time for relaxation. On top of the sundry gigs, the band was releasing a second album. To observers then, as now, the feat seemed remarkable. "Perhaps the most astonishing thing about *With the Beatles*," biographer Mark Hertsgaard asserts, "is that it was recorded at all. The Beatles were on the road virtually nonstop in 1963; recording sessions were squeezed in during one- or two-day stopoffs in London, songwriting sessions often took place in hotel rooms or in vans and buses while riding between gigs."[18]

The constant touring and recording, however, cemented the band as never before. Though the early Beatles had a similar type of unity in Hamburg—being foreigners bound together by their inability to speak German—they did not have the level of fame that would keep the Fab Four trapped in hotel rooms or on tour buses. George Martin noted, "The only peace they got was when they were alone in their hotel room, watching television and hearing the screams outside. That was about it. A hell of a life, really."[19] Yet, the Beatles in some ways thrived on the isolation. Forced to spend most of their days together, Lennon and McCartney's songwriting broadened into new topics, and Harrison continued to master his guitar. The media and fan attention was also something novel and exciting, especially to four men in their twenties. According to Alistair Taylor, Epstein's assistant who was with the band throughout their careers, "There was a real closeness between the boys in those heady early days. They felt like they were taking on the whole world and all they needed was each other."[20]

Indeed, the Beatles did take on the whole world in 1963 and 1964. On the heels of their success in the UK, the Beatles conquered America. They appeared on *The Ed Sullivan Show* in February 1964, and the craze of Beatlemania struck again—only this time to a viewing audience of 73 million people. In

The Beatles wave to thousands of screaming fans following their February 1964 arrival at Kennedy Airport in New York City.

America, the crowds outside the hotels where the Beatles stayed were larger, and the merchandising of the band's image—on everything from toys, to clothing, to Beatles wigs, to foods—was more pronounced. Still, the hysteria was just as it had been in England. And the same wave of Beatlemania followed the group as it toured Australia, the Netherlands, Denmark, Hong Kong, and Sweden in 1964. The schedule was demanding and fatiguing, but, as Mark Lewisohn notes, "Somehow, the Beatles accomplished all of this, and also recorded two albums, singles, and made a film."[21]

THE NEED TO ESCAPE

The Beatles' first film, *A Hard Day's Night*, was released in July 1964 and only added to Beatlemania. The decision to make a film, however, indicated that the Beatles were interested in more than just music. McCartney, at this time, began shooting little films of his own. Lennon was dealing with publishing giant Simon and Schuster, which wanted to print a collection of his stories. *In His Own Write* was published in 1964 and hit the best-seller list. A year later, a second volume, *A Spaniard in the Works*, was released. Much of this broadening of interests was a result of the band's recent relocation to London, the cultural mecca of 1960s England. There, the working-class Liverpudlians—who had abandoned their schooling years before—were exposed to art galleries, plays, movies, and the cultural elite who attended the same parties to which the Beatles were now invited. The influences were bound to rub off, and as Harrison recalls, "John and Paul went through their intellectual phase between 1963 and 1966. Looking back at John, he was always interested in poetry and films, but when we moved to London he and Paul got into a bit of one-upmanship over who knew the most about everything."[22] Rivalry had always characterized the Lennon-McCartney songwriting relationship, but the new intellectual one-upmanship was opening up new avenues of creative exploration, some of which Lennon and McCartney brought back to the band and some of which they monopolized for their own personal growth.

In 1964 and 1965, however, the Beatles could not devote much time to new pursuits. The demands of touring were all-consuming. Nineteen sixty-five began with a tour of Europe, and that was followed later in the year by a second tour of North America. The events were exhausting, and the band's playing and singing were suffering. Few observers seemed to notice, though, since most of the sounds generated from the stage were inaudible amongst the screams of the audiences. The depressing fact that they could not be heard was also getting to the band members, as was the imprisoning life of Beatlemania. The Beatles were eager to expand musically. Awed and motivated by the politically charged lyrics of folk-rocker Bob Dylan, who was emerging on the American scene, the Beatles wanted to ditch the hectic touring and focus on songwriting and studio recording. By the end of 1965, the enforced isolation of Beatlemania was no longer unifying, it was something from which the Beatles needed to escape.

FAREWELL TO BEATLEMANIA

In early 1966, the Beatles did take a break from touring. In April, they returned to the studio to record their most adventuresome record yet, *Revolver*. Having absorbed American music—from the folk rock of Dylan to the soul beat of Motown, the Beatles had obviously matured and were thinking beyond the pale of their earlier singles. In the words of critic Stephen Valdez, "The recording sessions for *Revolver* . . . demonstrate that the Beatles were concerned with creating studio art works rather than the dance-oriented pop songs that could readily be reproduced live."[23] The band was pleased with their first album not created in the midst of a tour schedule. Yet the Beatles still had commitments to fill. Brian Epstein had booked them on a tour of Japan and the Philippines, both of which proved disastrous. In the Philippines, the band was accused of slighting President Ferdinand Marcos and his wife by failing to visit the presidential palace. Angry mobs of Filipinos subsequently hounded the band, catcalling and physically assaulting the group as they fled the country.

Following on the heels of that tour was another scheduled set of dates in America. This new journey to the States began under the shadow of a remark John Lennon had made about the Beatles being more popular than Jesus Christ. Although Lennon tried to explain that the comment was taken out of context by the media, reaction in the American South and other conservative areas of the country was explosive. Religious groups held rallies in which Beatles albums were burned in retaliation for such perceived blasphemy. The

American tour, itself, was as dismal as its Asian predecessor. At a concert in Washington, D.C., members of the Ku Klux Klan protested outside the arena. And in Memphis, the band received death threats. Throughout the tour, the various venues were also failing to sell out as anticipated. The hysteria of the previous year had died down, and those fans who did show up to concerts were often disappointed by performances lasting only a half hour. Their final American concert was at San Francisco's Candlestick Park on August 29. After the show, the Beatles decided that their days of touring had come to an end.

IMPACT OF THE 1966 HIATUS

To some fans, the end of touring suggested that the Beatles were calling it quits as a band as well. Even the Beatles, themselves, had doubts. As their plane flew out of San Francisco, George Harrison remarked, "Well, that's it. I'm not a Beatle anymore."[24] In fact, after the American tour, the Beatles did go their separate ways for a time. Harrison went to India to indulge himself in the culture and especially the music of the subcontinent. Lennon took a starring film role in Richard Lester's *How I Won the War.* McCartney worked on a film score. And Starr stayed at home with his wife Maureen (whom he had married in 1965) and his infant son.

Though the hiatus was good for the bandmates, it was not promising for Brian Epstein. Recognizing the American tour would be the Beatles' last, Epstein understood that his role as concert arranger and promoter would come to an end. Unfortunately, that was Epstein's primary function in the Beatles industry. Epstein's assistant Alistair Taylor recalled:

> Brian was never quite the same after that tour. It took an awful lot out of him and I'm afraid his dependence on drugs of all prescriptions seemed to grow. . . . He would stay away from the office much more than ever before, for without the great tours to plan and undertake, he found his own personal workload cut down drastically. . . . I think he knew that the Beatles no longer needed him as much as they had needed him before. . . . I think he could see the end of his involvement.[25]

None of the Beatles knew of Epstein's depressive state, nor did they see Epstein as obsolete. Caught up in their individual projects, however, the Beatles did not contemplate Epstein's future; they simply reveled in their time away from Beatlemania.

In November 1966, the band returned to the studio. The

break had rejuvenated them and, especially for Harrison, brought new musical interests into the band's repertoire. The time away had also allowed the Beatles to indulge more in the culture of the late 1960s. As 1967's so-called summer of love rolled in, the Beatles embraced the change occurring among the young people in America, England, and western Europe. Anxious to dodge their Beatlemania images, the Fab Four ditched their lovable mop-top haircuts for long, unkempt hair, beards, mustaches, and sideburns. The matching suits were replaced by fanciful clothes that reflected the liberal hippie counterculture. And with image came the counterculture's touting of mind-expanding drugs. Adrift amid Indian music, drugs, and the playfulness of the hippie's libertine ethics, the band put together one of its defining albums—*Sgt. Pepper's Lonely Hearts Club Band.* The record showed the world that the Beatles were still on the cutting edge with young audiences, and, more importantly, it was a powerful creative statement that the band was still together and functioning as one.

THE LOSS OF A MANAGER AND FRIEND

To Brian Epstein, the experimental recording techniques and the scope of *Sgt. Pepper's* revealed that the Beatles were increasingly focused on what they could do in the studio—the one realm where Epstein had no pull or genuine interest. Epstein turned his attention to other bands and artists he had acquired over the years. Whether he did this begrudgingly or optimistically is not certain. In his autobiography, Epstein confesses, "Now that [the Beatles] are top of the world their challenge to me has diminished and I work better with a challenge than with a fait accompli."[26] Others such as Alistair Taylor and Hunter Davies believe that Epstein's diminished role was a nagging problem for someone whose livelihood was based on star making. Epstein's stable of other acts demanded his time, but none was successful in the way the Beatles had been, and therefore none was as fulfilling to Epstein. Whichever way he viewed his future, Epstein was still making big plans in August 1967. He was to appear as a guest emcee on a television show during an upcoming North American tour. He was also attending parties and seemed excited about his prospects. Having witnessed Epstein's jovial mood, most friends were taken unaware when on August 27, Epstein was found dead in his London home.

Epstein's death resulted from an overdose of Carbitral, a sleeping drug that contained bromide. Because Epstein often unwisely self-medicated, the cumulative effect of the bromide built up over the three days prior to his death proved fatal. The Beatles were not in England when Epstein's body was found. Two days earlier, they flew to India to seek spiritual guidance from the Maharishi Mahesh Yogi, a guru who had met the band in London. When George Harrison heard of Epstein's death, he said it was like an old-fashioned film "where they turn over the last page of one section to show you they've come to the end of it before going on to the next. That was what Brian's death was like. The end of a chapter."[27]

UNDER NO MANAGEMENT

As Brian Epstein had been so important in the making of the Beatles, his loss was equally important in their unmaking. Epstein had in many ways kept the band together, often acting as mediator in private squabbles and generally keeping the Fab Four on schedule for gigs and other projects. Each member knew they could look to Epstein to solve problems and to keep the band on track. When Epstein died, the Beatles did not try to replace him right away. Paul McCartney took over as the de facto manager primarily because no one else wanted the job. Ringo Starr had his family, George Harrison had his Indian mysticism, and John Lennon was in Hunter Davies's words "in a permanent state of mental abstraction,"[28] often listlessly hanging around his home watching television, barely interacting with his wife Cynthia. Under McCartney's direction, the band came together in late 1967 to put together a television movie called *Magical Mystery Tour.* The film's haphazard progress reflected the Beatles' own lack of administrative skills. With the band believing that— despite Epstein's loss—they could do anything, including manage and direct a feature, the four took on all responsibility. Quickly, the filming schedule mired, and the lack of a script and professional actors meant that most shoots were agonizing. The resulting film was quite amateurish and was lambasted by the press when it aired. "The year that began so positively ended on this decidedly negative note," Mark Lewisohn concludes. "*Magical Mystery Tour* proved that the Beatles were fallible, human even; Brian Epstein was dead, personal interests were tugging John, Paul, George, and Ringo in separate directions and internecine differences

The Beatles, performing onstage in 1967, are considered by many to be the most influential rock band of all time.

were taking root."[29] These differences would mark the final element in the band's decline over the next two years.

THE BEATLES IN CONTROL

In December 1967, the Beatles opened a clothing boutique in London. It was the first enterprise inaugurated under the Beatles' new company called Apple. The parent corporation was designed to indulge the band's whims. Having already conquered record making, the Beatles were eager to finance and produce other people's records—and other people's films, books, and whatever other intriguing schemes were brought to the band's doorstep at 94 Baker Street (and later, Saville Row). Although the Apple recording label became the Beatles' own label (distributed by Capitol Records in America and elsewhere by EMI) and produced some other interesting music, the corporation as a whole was shaky. None of the Beatles were experienced businessmen, and they didn't bother overseeing Apple's expenses or employees. Within eight months, the boutique closed its doors, having been a constant and unchecked drain on the Beatles' finances. Other parts of the business were equally ruinous. In just over a year from its inception, the Beatles were compelled to turn over the reins to a manager who could sort out the chaos and plug the monetary leak. Until then, the bandmates were mostly unconcerned with the financial failings of the venture and more interested in partaking of what the company offered—total control of their own music.

Beginning in the late spring of 1968, the Beatles began working on a new album (their ninth). Housed in a white jacket, the double album was officially called *The Beatles*, but nearly everyone referred to it simply as the White Album. In many ways, the White Album showed the Beatles getting back to what they did best—making music as a group. Although the band may have wanted to recapture the unity of purpose that seemed to crown *Sgt. Pepper's Lonely Hearts Club Band*, the White Album was worlds apart from that achievement. White Album biographer David Quantick asserts, "It is an album that has been described as the work of four solo musicians using each other as a backing band."[30]

The Beatles had complete creative control over the music; producer George Martin was now on the sidelines as a consultant—whose opinion was often ignored. Each Beatle took charge of the songs he added to the record, and while the band did play the core music (though not always together), the specific songwriter often assumed responsibility for the mixing and overdubbing of the tracks. Ringo Starr—never a prodigious contributor of songs to the Beatles' albums—was put off by the haphazard recording sessions. Often Starr would be called in to lay down a drum track and then be escorted out of the session when his part was finished. Sometimes Paul McCartney would take over the drumming to show Ringo exactly what he wanted in a song. The whole affair seemed insulting, and Starr walked out of the band temporarily—only to rejoin after being cajoled by the other members.

Without any single authority figure in control of the album, each of the principle songwriters—McCartney, Lennon, and Harrison—was unwilling to sacrifice any of his material to the greater good of the project. Instead of twelve or fourteen tracks making up the finished product, *The Beatles* had thirty songs spread over two LPs. Still, because the Beatles were the Beatles and the songwriting and musicianship were of Beatle quality, the White Album sold well.

YOKO ONO

While the creative and recording processes in making *The Beatles* were novel for the band, they were not as seriously disquieting to the composure of the band as was the presence of John Lennon's new love interest, Japanese avant-garde visual artist Yoko Ono. Lennon had met Ono at an art exhibit in May 1967, and he was taken with her unusual outlook on art, politics, and life. While Lennon's wife, Cynthia, had been a faithful companion, Ono provided the creative spark that reignited Lennon's imagination. Lennon became infatuated with Ono, believing her to be lover and muse. In May 1968, just prior to the main recording sessions for the White Album, Lennon and Ono collaborated on an album of their own called *Two Virgins.* The title conveyed Lennon's sense that his life was beginning anew—that real experience would take place in the company of Ono. When Cynthia Lennon found out about the pair (they made no secret about their relationship), she quietly filed for divorce and left the scene.

While Ono's arrival sounded a death knell for Lennon's marriage, it also produced a sour note in his relationship with the other Beatles. Ono began attending White Album recording sessions and then simply never left. Of course, being deeply in love, this was how Lennon wanted it, but his bandmates began seeing Ono's presence as an intrusion, perhaps since their wives and lovers had always remained patiently outside the studio confines. Lennon now sought counsel from Ono on his songs, and she even became the creative force behind "Revolution #9," the most unusual track on *The Beatles.* Nicholas Schaffner remarks that during the White Album sessions, "Yoko was never far from John's side; she would even follow him into the gent's room, and when she was ill, had a bed installed in the Beatles' recording studios. She thought she could be one of the boys."[51] But the other Beatles were not looking for a new member. In part, they were probably jealous of the time Ono was taking away from the band (and, in McCartney's case, from a personal and songwriting friendship). And in part, they were probably distrustful of how much influence Ono could bring to subsequent Beatles' albums.

NO CONSENSUS

Perhaps the most troublesome aspect of Lennon's and Ono's relationship was that it exacerbated the growing rift between Lennon and McCartney. The two boyhood chums who once worked on their songs together were now writing most of their material apart. And neither Lennon nor McCartney was clear on what was appropriate Beatles material. McCartney was still penning the more upbeat, innocuous tunes, and Lennon was delving into darker, personal themes that seemed to spring from the inspiration gained from his relationship with Ono. Both songwriters were, at this time, openly critical of each other's work—Lennon believing his new path was more true to himself as an artist, and McCartney concerned that Beatles' songs should be catchy enough to sell records. Outside of this debate sat George Harrison, who had become a better songwriter over time yet waited in vain to have his material receive the Beatles' stamp of approval. The debate over what material was ultimately suited for release was a sore spot with all three songwriters, leaving each feeling that his music might be better withheld for some future project.

By the time *The Beatles* was released in November 1968, the band's time together had shrunk mainly to studio recording. Gone were the Hamburg days or even the days of Beatlemania when the Fab Four were isolated and forced to rely on themselves for entertainment. Lennon spent most of his time with Ono staging performance art. Harrison was deeply into Indian music and was producing traditional recordings using Indian musicians. Starr was with his family but also appearing occasionally in films. Only McCartney seemed dedicated to moving the Beatles forward. Still trying to provide direction for the group, McCartney decided the Beatles should revive their live act. He set about organizing three concerts for December, ostensibly with the group's agreement. But as the time approached, the four could not agree on the venues or the format of the performances. The December shows were put on hold. As 1969 dawned, McCartney was still pushing his plan, but the nagging squabbles over the venue were now coupled with the other three members' waning enthusiasm for the project. Mark Lewisohn adds, "In a particularly dark mood one day John even suggested that the group simply call it quits and break up."[32] Registering his dissent with the concert plan, Harrison walked out of the practice sessions set up for the as-yet-to-be-decided performance date.

The rehearsals that Harrison left are known as the "Get

Back" sessions, named after the first single released from the period. The concept of sessions (and the proposed concert) was to leave behind the studio tricks displayed on *Sgt. Pepper's* and *The Beatles* and "get back" to the rock-and-roll sound that the band had somehow lost along the way. An album also entitled *Get Back* was to follow from the material put together for the concert. But neither the album nor the concert came to fruition. Even though Harrison returned to the project, no one proved very interested in its completion. "We just couldn't get into it," Lennon said later in a *Rolling Stone* interview. "And we put down a few tracks and nobody was in it at all."[33] When the band stopped the recording sessions, none of the members could be bothered to arrange or mix the album. The tapes were shelved along with the planned grand concert. Instead, the group assembled atop the Apple office building in Saville Row to give an impromptu performance of some of the material for crowds that gathered below. After this show of unity, the Fab Four went their separate ways for much of early 1969, fleeing from the internal strife and wondering if being a Beatle was still a worthwhile pursuit.

In June, the band reformed in the studio to record their final album. The sessions for *Abbey Road* were similar to those of the White Album. The four members were together for recording and then the individual Beatles mixed and overdubbed the tracks they composed. Somehow, the result seemed to bring back the glory of *Sgt. Pepper's*. But it was a short-lived golden moment. The band was already fracturing. Just prior to recording, Lennon, Harrison, and Starr agreed to allow Allen Klein, a tenacious accountant who had worked with other celebrities, to manage their finances. McCartney refused Klein's management and wanted to turn the resuscitation of Apple over to the firm of Eastman and Eastman, a New York legal and management partnership run by the father- and brother-in-law of McCartney's soon-to-be wife, Linda Eastman. For a time, both management firms handled different aspects of the Beatles, but eventually Klein fought for the lion's share. Klein reorganized Apple, transforming it from an experiment run by friends and hangers-on to an efficient corporation.

McCartney still believed Klein was trying to wheedle more out of the Beatles than just a simple management contract. In fact, Klein was now making all the decisions that

McCartney had been making over the past year, so some resentment was understandable. But McCartney did not press for Klein's removal. Instead, with his band mates against him, McCartney simply chose to stay away from the Apple offices and out of the public eye. Starr and Harrison joined him in avoiding the spotlight. Only Lennon remained visible at the end of 1969. With Yoko Ono, who was now Lennon's wife, the former leader of the Beatles was now leading another group, the newly formed Plastic Ono Band. The act played its first concert in September, leaving fans of the Beatles wondering if the Fab Four had split up—for good.

AND IN THE END

The demise of the Beatles came not with a bang, but with a whimper. By 1970, the four members had become four distinct personalities—each to varying degrees interested in acting, making music, producing other people's music, writing, and making artistic and political statements. In February, when BBC radio host David Wigg asked John Lennon what the future of the Beatles was, Lennon replied, "Well, each Beatle is doing his own thing at the moment, you know, and it could be a re-birth or a death and we'll see what it is. It'll probably be a re-birth, you know, for all of us."[54]

Lennon's comment reflected his own desire to break new ground apart from the Beatles, but it also contained a sense of goodwill for the other members. It was an odd sentiment considering the bickering that was plaguing each remaining meeting of the band. Yet, despite the ever-present tensions between the members—especially between Lennon and McCartney—the underlying friendship remained. Even in the most vitriolic letters written to McCartney at this time, Lennon often ended his tirade with "Love, John and Yoko." The Beatles had simply come through too much to forget that they had come through it together. McCartney summed up the feeling by saying, "No matter how much we split, we're still very linked. We're the only four people who've seen the whole Beatlemania bit from the inside out, so we're tied forever, whatever happens."[55] Each Beatle in his own words has echoed that sentiment in interviews from 1970 to the present, testifying to the power that held the friends together even as the band fell apart.

On April 9, 1970, Paul McCartney—the one who had the most optimism for the Beatles' future in its declining years—

officially announced that he was leaving the band. Unlike the previous times when Lennon, Harrison, and Starr had threatened to walk out of the band, none of the other Beatles persuaded McCartney to return. The following month, the posthumous *Let It Be* album was released. *Let It Be* was an unusual swan song for the Beatles. The album consisted of several tracks recorded for the unreleased *Get Back* LP, yet—as previously mentioned—remixed and rearranged by Phil Spector. Upon reviewing the record, *Rolling Stone* contended that Spector had transformed "the rough gems on the best Beatle album in ages into costume jewelry."[36] It would be nearly thirty-five years before Paul McCartney would try to reclaim those "gems" and show the world that even at their most dispirited moments, the Beatles were "a good little band."

Although McCartney's 2003 assessment of the Beatles on *Let It Be* reveals a false humility, the sentiment was not his alone. Throughout the group's career, John Lennon spoke of the Beatles as a little rock-and-roll band from Liverpool. Later in his life, George Harrison seconded Lennon's claim, and Ringo Starr emended it by stipulating that the Beatles were "a *really great* rock 'n' roll band."[37] Ultimately the fans will decide whether *Let It Be . . . Naked* will re-present the Beatles as "a good little band." More likely, however, any debate is moot. The Beatles were undeniably a powerful force in music. Their rise and fall as a group of friends and musicians is a fascinating story but not a story that is uncommon to the music world. It is their music that has come to entrance generation after generation of listeners. What *Let It Be . . . Naked* may prove is that four creative musicians could always come together as a band and make great, memorable music.

NOTES

1. Quoted in CBS News, "The Beatles Get Naked," November 14, 2003. www.cbsnews.com.

2. Nicholas Schaffner, *The Beatles Forever.* Harrisburg, PA: Cameron House, 1978, p. 6.

3. Hunter Davies, *The Beatles,* 2nd rev. ed. New York: W.W. Norton, 1996, p. 33.

4. Gareth L. Pawlowski, *How They Became the Beatles: A Definitive History of the Early Years, 1960–1964.* New York: E.P. Dutton, 1989, p. 9.

5. Quoted in Pawlowski, *How They Became the Beatles,* p. 33.

6. Davies, *The Beatles,* p. 79.

7. Brian Epstein, *A Cellarful of Noise: The Autobiography of the Man Who Made the Beatles.* New York: Byron Preiss, 1998, p. 98.

8. Epstein, *A Cellarful of Noise*, p. 98.

9. Pete Best and Patrick Doncaster, *Beatle!: The Pete Best Story.* London: Plexus, 2001, p. 133.

10. Mark Lewisohn, *The Complete Beatles Chronicle.* New York: Harmony, 1992, p. 52.

11. Epstein, *A Cellarful of Noise*, p. 125.

12. Lewisohn, *The Complete Beatles Chronicle*, p. 58.

13. Quoted in Pawlowski, *How They Became the Beatles*, p. 78.

14. The Beatles, *The Beatles Anthology.* San Francisco: Chronicle, 2000, p. 49.

15. Lewisohn, *The Complete Chronicle Beatles*, p. 88.

16. Davies, *The Beatles*, p. 180.

17. Davies, *The Beatles*, p. 181.

18. Mark Hertsgaard, *A Day in the Life: The Music and Artistry of the Beatles.* New York: Delta, 1995, p. 55.

19. Quoted in The Beatles, *The Beatles Anthology*, p. 155.

20. Alistair Taylor, *With the Beatles.* London: John Blake, 2003, p. 71.

21. Lewisohn, *The Complete Beatles Chronicle*, p. 137.

22. The Beatles, *The Beatles Anthology*, p. 109.

23. Quoted in Russell Reising, ed., *"Every Sound There Is": The Beatles' Revolver and the Transformation of Rock and Roll.* Burlington, VT: Ashgate, 2002, p. 89.

24. Quoted in Taylor, *With the Beatles*, p. 155.

25. Taylor, *With the Beatles*, pp. 155–56.

26. Epstein, *A Cellarful of Noise*, p. 197.

27. Quoted in Davies, *The Beatles*, p. 226.

28. Davies, *The Beatles*, p. lix.

29. Lewisohn, *The Complete Beatles Chronicle*, p. 239.

30. David Quantick, *Revolution: The Making of the Beatles' White Album.* Chicago: A Cappella Books, 2002, p. 12.

31. Schaffner, *The Beatles Forever*, p. 106.

32. Lewisohn, *The Complete Beatles Chronicle*, p. 306.

33. Quoted in Schaffner, *The Beatles Forever*, p. 117.

34. Quoted in Keith Badman, *The Beatles Off the Record: Outrageous Opinions and Unrehearsed Interviews.* London: Omnibus Press, 2000, p. 486.

35. The Beatles, *The Beatles Anthology*, p. 353.

36. Quoted in Schaffner, *The Beatles Forever*, p. 138.

37. The Beatles, *The Beatles Anthology*, p. 354.

CHAPTER 1

ORIGINS

THE BEATLES

The Quarry Men and the Silver Beatles

Gareth L. Pawlowski

In 1958, Allan Williams opened a small club on the premises of a former watch repair shop in Liverpool. The Jacaranda Club attracted the city's youth, who were interested in hearing the rock-and-roll bands that Williams signed up to play nightly. In 1959, Paul McCartney, John Lennon, George Harrison, and Stu Sutcliffe began frequenting the club and asking Williams if they could perform as the Quarry Men. Williams was taken with the earnest teenagers, despite their lack of polished musicianship, and allowed them to practice at the club. Williams became the group's unofficial agent and eventually allowed them to audition for an opening on a rock-and-roll tour of Scotland in 1960. On this tour, the group was rechristened the Silver Beatles to cash in on the "beat" group sound and image that was popular at the time.

In the following article, Beatles fan and collector Gareth L. Pawlowski recounts the origins of the Quarry Men and the Silver Beatles from their first meeting with Allan Williams to the post-tour doldrums of returning to Liverpool more experienced but no more famous.

Sometime during October 1959 four young men started coming to the Jacaranda. Their names were John Lennon, Paul McCartney, George Harrison, and Stuart Sutcliffe. They called themselves the Quarry Men and told [the club's owner Allan] Williams they were interested in playing at the Jacaranda. Williams said they could practice in the basement. His gesture was particularly generous since their primitive music was little more than noise. They were in fact just learning how to play their instruments. Paul and Stuart were trying to become bass players while John struggled to provide rhythm for George's guitar. The group had no drummer.

THE QUARRY MEN

Early in 1956 "Heartbreak Hotel" by Elvis Presley had topped the music charts in fourteen countries. Before Elvis, John Lennon was influenced by two other singers. Bill Haley's "Rock Around the Clock" hit England in 1955, and one year later Lonnie Donegan caused a lot of excitement with "Rock Island Line."

Elvis Presley was the most popular new sound to come along. Teenagers all over the world were mesmerized by this exciting new singer in America. And John Lennon was caught up in this wave. The most striking thing about this new music was the instrument used to produce it—the guitar. John knew that no formal musical training was necessary, because anyone could teach himself to play a few chords on a guitar.

John lived with his aunt, Mimi Smith, who did not approve of his choice of music, nor could she understand his obsession with the guitar. She repeatedly told him that "you'll never earn your living by it." So John visited his mother, Julia, and talked her into buying him a used guitar.

But John—age fifteen—wasn't thinking about music as a career. He was seeking a little fun and formed a skiffle group [playing skiffle, a form of British folk music]. Actually, it was simply a duo consisting of John and his schoolmate, Pete Shotton.

John named the two-man band the Quarry Men, after their school, the Quarry Bank High School.

No complete list exists naming all the boys who joined and left the Quarry Men. Paul McCartney became a member during October 1957. By early 1958 the group had grown to a quintet with John and Paul, plus Eric Griffiths (guitars), Len Garry (bass), and Colin Hanton (drums). George Harrison joined as another guitarist in March 1958.

By January 1960 the Quarry Men had evolved into a quartet consisting of John, Paul, George, and Stuart Sutcliffe.

Paul McCartney had been impressed by Bill Haley and His Comets, but he was not really awestruck until Elvis came along. He bought a guitar but had a difficult time getting any decent sounds from it. Finally, he realized the difficulty came from being left-handed and he had the guitar altered.

George Harrison was fourteen years old when he became interested in music. He had not been affected by American singers such as Frankie Laine and Johnnie Ray, but was impressed when he heard "Rock Island Line" by Lonnie Donegan's skiffle group. When Elvis arrived, he began teaching himself to play the guitar.

While Paul and George were attending the Liverpool Institute, Stuart Sutcliffe met John Lennon at the Liverpool College of Art. Stu, who couldn't play any instrument and was ignorant of popular music, was awed when he heard John, Paul, and George playing together. Stu was encouraged to buy a bass guitar and join the trio, who said they would teach him to play it. Stu eventually learned a few chords but his contribution as a musician was nil.

Although Elvis was everyone's idol, John, Paul, and George were also inspired by other American singers such as Gene Vincent, Buddy Holly, Little Richard, Jerry Lee Lewis, and Chuck Berry. Only two English singers had made names for themselves—Tommy Steele and Cliff Richard—and even they were unknown beyond Britain's shores.

KEEP PRACTICING

[The club's photographer] Cheniston Roland came to the Jacaranda one day and had his ears bombarded with an unusual musical cacophony. "What's all that bloody racket in the basement?"

"It's one of my groups, the Quarry Men," answered Williams. "You're not the first to complain, but they've got a sense of direction and I promised to get them some bookings when they improve."

Williams knew the four youngsters had *something* but their sound was shallow and unpolished.

"They kept asking me to find gigs for them," says Williams, "but I just told them to keep practicing."

When the Quarry Men weren't busy trying to improve their technique they would sit in the audience at the club, drink tea, and admire the music of Rory Storm and the Hurricanes—the number-one rock band in Liverpool. The group's drummer was a young man named Ringo Starr.

About this time, Williams was inspired with yet another enterprise that would interest local teenagers. After reading a London advertisement for the Chelsea Arts Ball, he decided he could sponsor the same type of affair locally. There had never been anything like it in Liverpool.

"You couldn't even find Liverpool on the tourist maps," says Williams. "There was no place where I could promote the local rock groups. So I decided to rent St. George's Hall. And that's how the first Liverpool Arts Festival was conceived."

It would also be the last.

The festival was scheduled to take place over a weekend. Cheniston adds: "the Liverpool Arts Festival gave rise to local talent that had been congregating in the clubs. It became a sort of focal point for all activities in the town, including sculptors, painters, pop groups, singers, and comics who were knocking around the clubs.

"I had an exhibition of photography. The displays were in the Everymans Theatre in the daytime and concerts were held in the evenings. In addition to the singers and other groups, political discussions were held along with poetry reading. Most of the people who ever amounted to anything from Liverpool got their start at the arts festival."

The Quarry Men were not allowed to perform at the festival because Allan Williams did not consider their musical ability worthy of exhibition. However, John, Paul, and George did contribute by constructing floats and assembling the artwork.

During the festival Cheniston befriended Stu Sutcliffe, the neophyte bass player. "He was more levelheaded," says Cheniston, "and a successful art student. Lennon was a failure at art school. Stuart would come over to my shop and talk about pictures and composition."

The arts festival was killed, recalls Cheniston, when "some local college kids went up to the galleries and threw flour and foam from fire extinguishers onto the floor below. Things got out of hand and a big melee broke out. Of course, the Liverpool council wasn't too pleased and made sure it would not happen again."

Throughout the early months of 1960 the spirits of all the local rock groups were at a low ebb. Their days were spent sulking at the Jacaranda Club, where discussion centered on the ill-fated festival. They had been given a taste of performing on stage to excited audiences. Now it was all over. They went to Williams with pleas for him to find them some engagements. Williams had begun to let the boys perform in the evenings at the Jacaranda. Their music, however, was still amateurish, and audiences were not responsive.

Then Allan Williams heard about a rock show at the Liverpool Empire produced by London talent agent Larry Parnes. "The show starred Gene Vincent," says Williams. "I wanted to see what the reaction would be from the teenagers, so I bought a ticket and went inside. When Gene Vincent came on stage the girls in the audience screamed and went wild. I said to myself that I could put on a bigger show and give the local bands a chance to be on stage with known rock 'n' roll groups."

Williams began organizing the "Greatest Show Ever to Be Staged" in Liverpool, produced under the banner of "Jacaranda Enterprises, by arrangement with Larry Parnes." The three-hour program would star Gene Vincent and Eddie Cochran and feature local bands.

Although listed at the bottom of the bill, Rory Storm and the Hurricanes, Cass and the Cassanovas, and other Liverpool groups would get their first chance to appear in a big rock show.

Once again, however, John, Paul, George, and Stu were excluded. Owing to the response (or nonresponse) from customers at the Jacaranda, Williams did not feel confident of their ability and thought their playing was still too unpolished for the paying public. He told them to keep practicing.

THE SILVER BEATLES GET AN AUDITION

Two weeks before the show Larry Parnes called Williams from London with tragic news. Eddie Cochran had just been killed in an auto accident. Although Gene Vincent had also been in the car and had suffered a leg injury, he agreed to perform. Parnes suggested that the show be canceled. Williams disagreed, explaining that the kids in his bands were all keyed up and he didn't want to disappoint them. The show would go on as scheduled.

On May 3 the big event took place in Liverpool Stadium. This time it was Larry Parnes's turn to sit in the audience watching an Allan Williams production.

John, Paul, George, and Stu were also watching.

Afterward, Parnes had a long talk with Williams and expressed his admiration for the groups from Liverpool. He wanted to hire a couple of bands to back one of his artists for a tour in Scotland.

Three days later a letter from Mark Forster, one of Parnes's assistants, arrived at the Jacaranda Club. The letter stated that "Duffy Power will be touring Scotland from June 2nd to 11th inclusive . . . and Johnny Gentle will be touring Scotland from June 16th to 25th. For these two periods, as agreed, we are willing to pay your groups £120.0d plus the fares from Liverpool. . . . Should you agree to these suggestions we will arrange for both Duffy and Johnny, who incidentally is a Liverpool boy, to travel up to Liverpool to rehearse with your groups towards the end of May."

The letter continued: "We will make arrangements for Mr. Parnes to come and audition your groups to select the most suitable. He will also bring Billy Fury as Billy will want one of these four groups for his own personal use. Incidentally, the idea of Billy wanting a group from his own hometown will provide several interesting press stories and publicity tie-ups."

The groups chosen by Williams to compete for this tour were Gerry and the Pacemakers, Cass and the Cassanovas, Cliff Roberts and the Rockers, Derry and the Seniors . . . and the newly renamed Silver Beatles. At last, Williams felt that the boys were ready to demonstrate their musical abilities.

Lennon was very excited because Billy Fury was a local boy who had made it big, and the possibility of backing him dominated John's thoughts.

The Silver Beatles practiced every day. Although they had no drummer, the problem was solved by arranging for a stand-in at the audition.

When the big day came the boys were very tense. This could prove to be their first big break or a monumental disappointment.

The Jacaranda was not large enough to hold the auditions but this presented no problem to Williams. He had recently leased the Wyvern Social Club at 108 Seel Street and was having it converted into his latest venture, the Blue Angel Club.

May 10 was a beautiful sunny morning as the bands wandered into the Wyvern Club. The musicians wore stylish suits, carried expensive instruments, and were well known locally. Suddenly, the Silver Beatles felt out of place in their jeans, sweaters, and tennis shoes. Their distressed mood, however, was overshadowed by a more serious dilemma. The drummer they had hired wasn't there.

Upon the arrival of Billy Fury, Larry Parnes, and Mark Forster, the auditions got under way. Parnes and Fury watched with little enthusiasm as each band—first Cass and the Cassanovas, then Derry and the Seniors, then Gerry and the Pacemakers—played several rock classics. During a break in the auditions, John Lennon, spellbound from being in the presence of a star, approached Fury with a slip of paper and asked for an autograph. . . .

After the break, Cliff Roberts and the Rockers had their turn. Finally, it was time for the Silver Beatles. When Parnes learned that their drummer had failed to show up, Johnny Hutchinson, drummer for Cass and the Cassanovas, reluctantly agreed to sit in. Hutchinson was one of the most talented drummers among the Merseyside bands [that is, bands from cities along the Mersey River]. The fact that he would help the Silver Beatles must have come from some irrepressible urge to do a good deed, because he openly regarded the boys as slovenly dressed unknowns whose musical talents "weren't worth a carrot."

Mark Forster looked at Lennon and asked for the group's name.

"Silver Beatles," answered John. This was the first time they'd ever had a chance to use it.

John, Paul, and George went into a rowdy number while Stu stood with his back to the judges. The routine drum beat from Hutchinson made him look like a computer-programmed robot.

Parnes and Fury immediately noticed the difference in style from the previous contestants. When John sang an Elvis song, Williams became annoyed at workmen who were banging away and ordered them to stop until the auditions were finished.

After they had performed a couple of songs, their rent-a-drummer, Tommy Moore, arrived. Moore had been collecting his drum kit from another club on the other side of town.

When the boys had completed their repertoire, Billy Fury looked at Parnes and said, "This is the group, the Silver Beatles."

Parnes agreed that they were the most interesting of the groups, but noticed that Stu Sutcliffe had been trying to hide his lack of ability. Parnes turned to Williams. "Allan, can you get them to play something without the bass player?"

A lump suddenly formed in Williams's throat. He was not prepared for this, but a request from Larry Parnes could not be denied. Williams asked the boys to do a number without Stu.

Lennon objected. "We're a group, all or none. That's the way it is."

Parnes was not anxious to provoke an argument and did not pursue the matter. He told Williams the group would be accepted if they changed their minds about the bass player.

The Silver Beatles stood by Stu.

When the auditions were over, Williams, Parnes, and the others went to the Jacaranda to celebrate. . . .

The First Tour

Allan Williams was aware that the Silver Beatles were sounding better every day. And they kept pestering him for gigs.

"I decided to become their manager," says Williams, "but first I had to find a drummer. . . . I asked Brian Cassar [Cass of Cass and the Cassanovas] if he knew a good drummer. He suggested Tommy Moore, who had played with the boys at the Wyvern audition. He said that Tommy worked at the Garston Bottle Works. I went and found him at the bottle company and offered him a job with the Silver Beatles. He climbed down from the forklift and accepted."

Conflict arose from the start between John Lennon and Tommy Moore. They did not like each other. Tommy, at thirty-six, was much older than nineteen-year-old John. As weeks passed John kept up a continual stream of caustic remarks aimed at Tommy and threatened to dampen the team spirit of the group.

Williams had been sending some of his groups on the road and now he felt the Silver Beatles were ready. He arranged for them to back Johnny Gentle on the Scotland tour, the dates of which had been moved up to May 20–28.

Before setting off for their first professional tour the boys had to get excused from their daily routines. Lennon and Sutcliffe concluded that the art college wouldn't miss them and decided simply to skip classes. Harrison had already quit school to work as an apprentice electrician and was able to get his vacation early. McCartney, always a politician, slick-talked his father into believing that the Liverpool Institute had granted all students a two-week holiday to prepare for exams.

Tommy Moore faced the most difficult task—that of persuading his girlfriend that he'd come back with a lot more money than his paycheck from the bottle works.

Johnny Gentle was shocked upon meeting the Silver Beatles. They wore black jeans and black T-shirts and appeared as if they had been sleeping in them for weeks. Also, they had no amplifiers for their electric guitars.

While driving to Scotland, with Gentle at the wheel, the van hit an automobile. The Silver Beatles were shaken but uninjured—except for the drummer. Tommy Moore had been struck in the mouth by an instrument case and lost his front teeth. He was taken to a local hospital while the group continued onward to their first engagement.

The manager at the club inquired about the drummer's absence and was told about the accident. He was sympathetic but insisted on a drummer.

John went back to the hospital and ordered Tommy to get out of bed and fulfill his obligation. The injured drummer finally agreed but was in pain throughout the tour. Lennon took advantage of this in a cruel manner by relentlessly tormenting Tommy while onstage.

When the tour was completed Tommy had suffered enough physical pain from his injury along with the constant abuse from Lennon. He returned to his job at the bottle works.

The Silver Beatles found another drummer, a man named Norman Chapman.

The Scotland tour had been the Silver Beatles' baptism in show biz and they had been elated to see their name, although in small print, on advertising posters.

After returning to Liverpool, however, they were back at square one. Most of their time was spent loafing at local coffee bars and they were lucky if they got two gigs a week.

On May 20, while the boys were in Scotland, Allan Williams had met with Les Dodd, head of Paramount Enterprises. Dodd arranged for the Silver Beatles to appear with Gerry and the Pacemakers on June 6 at Grosvenor Hall. They received £10; £1 went to Williams as their manager and £1 to the bouncer, leaving each member of the band with about $4.50 U.S.

Four days earlier the Silver Beatles had appeared at the Neston Institute in Wirral, but they were called the Beatles in a review by the *Heswell and Neston News and Advertiser.*

When Norman Chapman put on an army uniform for two years of required national service, the group was once again without a drummer. Many times they tried to lure Tommy Moore back for their occasional engagements. One evening, while Tommy was working the night shift, they stopped at the bottle works on their way to a gig. Tommy completely ignored their pleas. Another time they went to his apartment, but had to cope with Tommy's girlfriend. She was still losing sleep over the paltry pay he had earned for the Scotland tour and was absolutely livid about the bill from Tommy's orthodontist. She had two words for the group: "Piss off!"

During this desolate time the Silver Beatles' only regular job was playing background music for a stripper named Janice in a club partly owned by Allan Williams. The boys were paid ten shillings per week to provide sultry guitar chords as Janice wiggled and writhed for an audience of drunken sailors and panting businessmen.

ON TO HAMBURG

And there they might have stayed if one of Williams's other acts—a steel band—hadn't run out on him. "I went to the Jacaranda one evening," says Williams, "to see if the Caribbean Steel Band was [still] there. I had received letters from other [club owners] asking me to let them perform in their clubs, but refused. Steel bands were very scarce in England at the time. Well, to my surprise, the steel band was gone!"

A few days later, Williams received a letter from the band, who had skipped town and gone to Hamburg in West Germany. "They told me how great it was and that I should open a club there. I wondered what Hamburg had to offer so I went there and paid a visit to several clubs. The bands were German rock groups and were lousy. I knew my Liverpool bands were better and the people would go wild over them.

"When I got back to Liverpool I found out that Derry and the Seniors were unhappy with their payment on various gigs and had gone to London to get even with their promoter. I went along to make sure they didn't get into trouble. While there I went to the Two I's Bar in Soho and ran into Bruno Koschmider, a Hamburg nightclub owner. I reminded him about my group. We agreed on terms and drew up a contract. The first band I ever sent to Hamburg was Derry and the Seniors."

The Silver Beatles were constantly asking Williams about going to Hamburg. "I finally decided they were good enough," says Williams, "but again faced a never ending problem. No drummer. And this is when Pete Best became a Beatle."

"Making Show" in Hamburg

Pete Best and Patrick Doncaster

Drummer Pete Best joined the Beatles in 1960, not long after the band had dropped "Silver" from its name. Best's mother owned a small Liverpool club called the Casbah at which the Silver Beatles had appeared. The band—which previously had relied on a series of stand-in drummers—needed a permanent drummer to join them for an upcoming tour of Hamburg, Germany. Paul McCartney knew Best from the club, and he heard that Best had just gotten a new drum kit, so he phoned to ask if Pete would be interested in taking on the job. After a quick audition, Pete Best became the first drummer of the fledgling Beatles.

Allan Williams, who was now managing the Beatles, signed a contract in August 1960 with Bruno Koschmieder to send the band to Hamburg. Koschmieder owned the Kaiserkeller and the Indra clubs in Hamburg and hoped to attract customers by featuring the beat group sound that was becoming very popular in Germany. Before the contract was even signed the Beatles were on the Continent. It was an eye-opening experience for the bandmates. Hamburg was a world apart from drab Liverpool. The Reeperbahn—the locale of the Kaiserkeller—was filled with strip joints and rough nightclubs. The Indra, just off the Reeperbahn, was not nearly as exciting. In the following excerpt from his autobiography (cowritten by Patrick Doncaster), Pete Best describes the Beatles' arrival at the Indra and their initial disappointment at finding it "as lively as a cemetery chapel." Best goes on, however, to say that because the band did not have to live up to the expectations of a large, paying crowd, the Beatles felt free to play what they wanted, how they wanted—more to entertain themselves rather than the audience. Wild stunts and frantic, loud playing were encouraged by Koschmieder who only asked in awkward English that the Beatles "make show." The stage-show zaniness that the Beatles displayed on this and subsequent tours of German nightclubs became part of the band's charm in later years, even after the rest of the Beatles dropped Best from their lineup.

There was, it seemed, a right end and a wrong end of the Grosse Freiheit. The right end was immediately off the Reeperbahn itself and was a small-scale continuation of the neon world of sex, clubs and music. As you progressed along the Grosse Freiheit the lights and the attractions gradually dwindled until you found yourself at the wrong end, which was as dull as a morgue and about as inviting. This was where someone had decided to place the Indra. Our excitement began slowly to ebb away when Bruno [Koschmieder] showed us the club. It was about as lively as a cemetery chapel. The lighting was gloomy, but there was just enough of it to see that there were only two people in the place. Nothing was happening on the stage and a jukebox stood forlornly silent. It looked as if it would take a miracle to get even St Vitus to dance in here. We felt dejected and looked at each other with faces that reflected our growing misery.

'Is it open?' I asked Bruno lightheartedly, not wanting to believe that this depressing dump was to be where the Beatles were to burst on to the great German public. Hamburg had a population of more than a million and a half people, but only two of them had forced themselves to walk downstairs off the cobbles and into the Indra.

Bruno treated us to what for him was a smile. 'You boys will make the Indra into another Kaiserkeller,' he said. 'No one comes to this place,' he admitted, stating the obvious. 'But you'll make it go when you make show.'

'Make show' . . . that was a phrase we were going to have to learn to live with for a long time. Bruno, in his halting English, pronounced it 'mack show', which didn't strike us as being all that amusing as we stood there like sacks of potatoes with our suitcases in hand. . . .

On the opening night at the Indra a reasonable crowd turned up to cast a critical eye on the new boy wonders from

Liverpool. Acoustically, it was like playing under a pile of bedclothes. There were drapes everywhere—probably because the Indra had once been a strip club—and they killed the sound in its tracks. We took to the stage in the depths of depression. Bruno, very much in evidence, yelled at us that we must 'make show', which we did, more as a release for our mounting anger rather than to please him.

'All the way from Liverpool to leap around like a lot of idiots!' Lennon summed up. For that's what 'making show' was all about—jumping around aimlessly, stamping, writhing on the floor. None of us had ever acted the fool like this on stage before.

Hitherto, groups had generally stood and played somewhat in the style of Cliff Richard's Shadows, with their neat little coordinated footsteps and gentle swaying, which was never allowed to get in the way of the music. Of course there had been the cavortings of Bill Haley and his Comets, jumping around or lying on their backs still playing their instruments, which had all seemed a bit daft, and the piano gymnastics of Jerry Lee Lewis, who exploded like a firework in his act. But it wasn't for us.

Anyway, our repertoire was not exclusively rock'n'roll and we were playing several middle-of-the-road offerings. Paul was into *Somewhere over the Rainbow* and other syrupy numbers. We used to do *Red Sails in the Sunset* and *Ain't She Sweet.* No wonder when the time came a lot of major record companies slammed the door in our faces. But this was the start and we had a lot to learn. 'Make show', Bruno had ordered with his usual Germanic charm. So we did. Like five bloody lunatics.

We went from one extreme to the other. John and Paul were the looniest. John did his best to imitate Gene Vincent, grabbing up the microphone as if he were going to lay into the audience with it, carrying it around with him, leaping about with it like a maniac. Paul roared around screaming like Little Richard and, as the days passed, an act developed.

Stu behaved something like a puppet and managed to hold on to the sort of James Dean image he had fostered, quietly trying to stay cool in the background behind his dark shades. There was not much I could do from behind the drums other than stand up and hop around the kit with a tom-tom under my arm. George paid serious attention to his guitar-playing, trying to prevent the sets from becoming too ridiculous.

MAKING SHOW

The German rockers loved it and no one realized—least of all Bruno—that we were trying to take the piss out of them. But in the end it worked against us. This was the Beatles developing, creating excitement. 'Making show' would eventually take us over. However, at first it was a protest for the treatment we were receiving, letting ourselves rip because of the lousy digs and the sub-survival wages of £15 a week each.

We had one number we used to put in that began very slowly and sounded like smooch music. The audience would take to the floor and get all cuddly and close, then suddenly we would erupt into a frenzied rock tempo. At first it took the Germans by surprise—to us it was another form of protest—but then they started to request the song where we changed gear in mid-stream! Another backfire.

We used to stomp around half crazed for more than seven hours a night. Making show? You've never seen anything like it. Sometimes Paul wouldn't even have his guitar plugged in, but no one noticed the omission with all the noise that went on. John used to roll around on stage when he wasn't throwing the mike in the air; then he would twist himself into a hunch-back pose. By way of a change he would jump on to Paul's back and charge at George and Stu and send them reeling. Sometimes they would give each other piggy-backs. What little music there was would be made by George and Stu and most of that was simply rhythm. Other times John would hurl himself into a sort of flying ballet leap from the stage into the audience and end up doing the splits.

While the audience was dancing, John and Paul often jumped down from the stage and bundled into them like wild bulls; or maybe they would do a ring-of-roses with them. But this is what the punters wanted and had paid money for. They didn't want to sit around and listen to original Beatles' music—not that a lot of it existed at this stage—and it was obvious that they appreciated the outrageous slapstick rather than the musicianship. They started to call us the *beknakked* Beatles—a German slang word that described us as the mad or crazy Beatles—but we never stopped to worry about it.

The songs were exclusively American; Fats Domino and Carl Perkins numbers, along with Gene Vincent, Elvis and Little Richard hits. The Germans loved the Ray Charles classic *What'd I Say*, which really lent itself to audience participation. They would echo the lyrics and keep time to the beat, banging their bottles on the tables.

Many of the stories that have been told over the years about the way we used to behave on stage allege that the Beatles used to have serious fights in front of the audiences. This wasn't strictly true: a lot of it was just part of 'making show'. What used to appear to be a brawl on stage began at

---

OUR APPRENTICESHIP

George Harrison remembered the time spent on tour in Germany as the Beatles' apprenticeship. In Hamburg's clubs, the band had the time to continually rehearse material and experiment with songs that might not have been popular back in England.

In my opinion our peak for playing live was in Hamburg because at that time we weren't famous. So the people who came to see us were drawn in by the music or by whatever atmosphere we created. Also, at that time, with us being from Liverpool, it was a big scene because people would always say, "You've got to be from London to make it." They always thought we were hick or something. But when we played in Hamburg, they kept wanting us back because we would pull in lots of people.

We first went to a place called the Indra, which was shut down. Then we went to the Kaiserkeller, and then the Top Ten, which was probably the best club on the Reeperbahn. At that time it was really fantastic. There was echo on the microphones and it was really a gas. So we'd go in there and spend afternoons rooting through all those old songs like, you know, "Money," and all the sort of tunes that weren't popular particularly but were quite heavy. We'd do all those ones by Chuck Berry and Little Richard, all the rock-and-roll things. We just kept doing that, even though that sort of period had died out.

The Hamburg days, in retrospect, were probably the most important times of our lives because it was what you could call our apprenticeship. We worked very hard and we worked long hours. We played for eight hours a night, seven days a week for over four and a half months on our first go-round there. We really got a lot of material down, a lot of material we would never have learned if we hadn't gone there. It was one great rehearsal and it really got the group going. Yes, those days were very important to The Beatles.

David Pritchard and Alan Lysaght, *The Beatles: An Oral History.* New York: Hyperion, 1998.

the Indra, where nightly we began to take more liberties in the cause of 'making show'. Paul, with possibly only one string on an unplugged guitar, would rush up to John while he was singing and pretend to butt him. Feigning anger, Lennon would retaliate. It must have all appeared to be very real to the patrons and used to wind them up, but it was sheer pretence, a mock battle in which nobody was hurt. In those early days we were extremely close and the best of friends at all times and we would go through much together in the spirit of five rather seedy musketeers.

There is no doubt that John and Paul gave their all to 'making show'—even if they did find it a release from the frustrations besetting us all. Lennon gradually became bolder with each week that passed, haranguing the paying customers as 'f—ing Krauts', or Nazis or Hitlerites. Later he extended this repertoire of venom to 'German spassies' (spastics), indulging in his obsession with the disabled which would later manifest itself more publicly in his writings, drawings and statements during interviews. For their part, the Germans, whom he also advised to 'get up and dance, you lazy bastards!', rarely showed any signs of understanding and would often applaud his insults.

Indulging his cripple fantasies on stage, he would twist himself into grotesque shapes which were far more comprehensible and which not everyone in the audience appreciated. But what other people thought of Lennon rarely caused him concern. Yet the mere sight of deformed or disabled people sickened him physically and he could never bear to be in their company. More than once I was with him in a Hamburg cafe when suddenly he would discover that the occupant of a nearby table was a war veteran, minus a limb or disfigured in some way. John would leap up from his seat and scurry out into the street. On one occasion I saw this happen even after he had already ordered a meal and was about to be served.

He never tried to explain this odd behaviour or his reasons for devoting so much of his artistic talent to depicting distorted characters. Somewhere deep down I felt that perhaps he nursed a sort of sadness for them.

THE BEATLE BUZZ

More and more people were now seeking their entertainment at the Indra as the news of the mad, bad Beatles buzzed through the city. Within a month we had become a hit group with our interpretation of 'making show', with its sham fights, crazy horse-play and John's earthy advice.

He gave many people in the audiences the impression that he was a buffoon, but what he did on stage was simply a form of escapism for him. He played the idiot who shouted his mouth off and yelled obscenities but was the outright victor in any slanging match. It was the kind of behaviour they came to expect of him. After these bitter attacks on the people who were paying our wages Lennon would simmer down as though he had just aired some long pent-up grievance and was relieved to have got it off his chest.

I used to try and explain this abuse of audiences to myself but could only conclude that John harboured no deep hatred of the Germans and that they were simply the scapegoats for his increasing frustration at having to entertain them in a fashion that really wasn't his style.

At the Indra we acquired a friend who would stand by the Beatles for a long time to come. She was the lavatory attendant, a lady whom we christened Mutti. Anyone over the age of twenty seemed old to us, but I reckon Mutti must have been in her fifties, hence our nickname for her, sounding something like the German word for mother—*Mutter*. She was in nightly attendance backstage, where our poky dressing room adjoined the toilets (where else?). When we came off stage she would be waiting for the perspiring Beatles with towels and paper napkins and changes of shirt, which was very necessary after the rigours of 'making show'.

Almost nightly as well she had to prepare a needle and thread for John to repair his pants after his dare-devil Nureyev leaps. But he always insisted on making his own renovations, just sitting there in his underpants, sewing away and using something like sailor's tacks and a few reef knots. (Needless to say the repair would give way after the next performance!) If anyone arrived backstage—male or female—while he was working away in his underwear he would simply invite them to 'come in and make yourself at home' and continue with the task.

By this time we were drinking more than our fair share of Hamburg's booze. It came by the crate and we drank on stage, as well as clowned. The Germans were extremely generous and recognized that 'making show' could create an enormous thirst. Some of the dedicated regulars were ever deserting the Kaiserkeller now to catch the Beatles at the Indra. Not that Bruno minded. We were giving him what he wanted and achieving his objective for the Indra—to make it as popular as his other club.

If there had been any rivalry, it all ceased two months after we first opened at the Indra, when Bruno gave us the news: 'The Indra's got to close!' 'Why?' we inquired anxiously. 'Because of the noise!' we were informed. We were all disappointed and confused. We had worked like maniacs to build the club up from nothing—and now it was going to shut down due to the din of 'making show'! It was ironic. Apparently Koschmieder had been warned several times by the police that the Indra would have to close if the noise continued. He ignored them and we carried on blissfully unaware of the threat. He knew, however, that the police would eventually lose patience, and he had warned us only just in time.

MOVING TO THE KAISERKELLER

The end came very suddenly after Bruno's announcement. We arrived one night as usual to find that the Indra had been closed by the cops. Bruno was obviously more annoyed than we were, but there was nothing he could do about it. Residents living opposite or nearby the club at this wrong end of the Grosse Freiheit had been complaining bitterly and the madness had to cease—by order. Yet strangely an old lady who lived directly above the club in an apartment never did moan to the police. She was either deaf or a latter-day rocker.

Even if this was the end of the Indra it was by no means the end of the Beatles in Hamburg. Bruno, who was now openly pleased at the results of our endeavours, wasn't prepared to let us go that easily (our initial contract with him was for two months and could be extended verbally). He decided to move us along the street to the Kaiserkeller and thus help pack more people in. Here John would be able to improve on his ballet act. The Kaiserkeller boasted a piano on stage and he would climb on top of it, stomp around, then fling himself with a sensational leap into the customers.

Somehow the Kaiserkeller seemed to bring out the best and worst in Lennon. One night he appeared on stage in his underpants in a knockabout impression of Hitler, a toilet seat round his neck, a broom for martial effect and chanting '*Sieg heil! Sieg heil!*' If anyone objected to what he was doing they would be told to get stuffed. Sometimes the rest of us used to enter into the spirit by daring him to be even more outrageous.

As winter approached at the Kaiserkeller he bought himself a baggy pair of long johns in an effort to keep warm. Late one Saturday night when he was sitting in them in his lousy room behind the Bambi Kino, writing a letter to [his girlfriend] Cynthia, George said: 'I dare you to go out and stand in the Grosse Freiheit in those!'

Lennon didn't hesitate. He picked up an English newspaper he had been reading earlier, tucked it under one arm, kicked open the crash doors, strode out into the middle of the street—crowded with weekend visitors to St Pauli—and just stood there reading the paper.

Then, after several minutes, he folded it, put it under his arm again, came to attention with a Nazi click of the heels, gave the Hitler salute, said goodnight in German to the onlookers and marched back inside with a deadpan face. Paul, George and I watched the whole episode, peering round the edge of the doorway, but John never received any reward from us when he carried through one of our dares.

I can't remember which one of us challenged him to bare his bottom on stage. The bandroom at the Kaiserkeller was near the entrance and to get to the stage we had to walk through the audience. This night John changed into a pair of navy-blue swimming trunks and marched straight-faced to the stand with his guitar. In the middle of *Long Tall Sally* he turned round and, with his back to the audience, dropped his trunks to reveal all.

His rear was only a foot away from the customers, so close that they could have kissed his ass. But no one did. There was some laughter but no comment at all from the Kaiserkeller patrons.

When we opened there we doubled on the bill with Derry and the Seniors. Later we were reunited with our old pal Rory Storm, who still had this fellow Ringo Starr drumming for him with the Hurricanes. It was on this first trip to Hamburg that he and I really got to know each other. Drummers tend to pal up and talk about their trade and equipment. This happened in a minor way in England before we went to Germany, when we both attended a memorial show for Eddie Cochran at Liverpool Stadium. But it was in Germany that the friendship blossomed.

We reached the stage where we would lend one another drumsticks and go shopping together for items of kit such as cymbals. It was an extremely pleasant relationship that would last for a long time to come, but not for always.

CHAPTER 2

SUCCESS

THE BEATLES

"Love Me Do" Takes Off

Alistair Taylor

After recording four demo tracks for Parlophone, neither the Beatles nor their manager, Brian Epstein,
had heard anything from George Martin, the label's
A&R man. The band continued to tour locally to
larger and larger audiences. Then, on August 16,
1962, while the band's reputation was at a high point,
Brian Epstein called drummer Pete Best to his offices.
During the meeting, Epstein told Best that he was no
longer a Beatle. When Best asked why, Epstein said
that George Martin had not liked his style and that
the other Beatles felt he did not fit in anymore. (Martin later denied having influenced the decision to fire
Best.) Without seeing his bandmates again, Best
silently but acrimoniously left the group. He was replaced by Ringo Starr, the former drummer of Rory
and the Hurricanes, another Liverpool act.

With the new lineup, George Martin contacted the
band to come and rerecord some of its demo songs
for an official-release single. In September, John,
Paul, George, and Ringo visited EMI studios in London on two separate occasions to perform several
numbers. Of those songs recorded, Martin chose
"Love Me Do" and "P.S. I Love You" for the band's
first single. The next month the single was released
and achieved success, peaking in December at number seventeen in the British *Record* retailer chart. Alistair Taylor, who served as Brian Epstein's assistant
at the time, recalls in the following selection from
his autobiography how the Beatles' first single
launched the band on its path toward fame. Taylor
remembers how Martin was eager to follow up the
first single's success by having the band record a
tune written by a veteran songwriter. As Taylor
notes, however, the Beatles insisted that they could
write their own hit material as they had done with

> "Love Me Do." Eventually, another original hit single
> and a first LP followed, and the Beatles' success
> seemed assured.

'Love Me Do' changed everything. The first record might
have peaked at a modest 17, but it launched the group on to
a new level and it registered their astonishing ability to
shrewd observers. The Beatles were suddenly wanted on
television on Granada's *People and Places* which was a re-
gional programme for the north that went out from Manchester. The Beatles went down well and then had to dash
off to Hamburg for two previously booked fortnights of live
appearances. The whirlwind of excitement was really starting to blow at the time. Brian was on a permanent high. The
boys kept coming into the [NEM record] shop [where Epstein and Taylor worked], as if there were going to be daily
bulletins on their rise to super stardom.

George Martin was pleased with the success but totally
won over to Brian's view that the boys had it in them to be
something very special. The most important task was to find
a follow-up record which would build on the sales of 'Love
Me Do'.

[Songwriter] Mitch Murray sent in a catchy little song to
George Martin called 'How Do You Do It?' George thought it
was definite hit material. The Beatles tried it out and hated
it. Gerry Marsden couldn't agree less and turned it into a
number-one hit. The boys didn't regret their decision. 'Lots
of shit rises to the top of the charts,' observed John laconi-
cally one night. 'We don't do shit.'

There was a lot of rivalry between the groups in those
days. Gerry felt with some justification that Brian concentrated all his efforts on the Beatles and the boys frankly
thought they were a whole lot better than Gerry and the
Pacemakers. When the Beatles rejected 'How Do You Do It?'
George Martin was annoyed and told them that if the song
wasn't good enough for them then they had better come up
with something that was acceptable. And quickly.

THE SONG THAT CHANGED EVERYTHING

'Please, Please Me' was the Beatles response to the challenge. It was the song that changed everything. It was released on 11 January 1963 and by 22 February it was num-

ber one. Admittedly, it initially shared the prized top spot with Frank Ifield's 'The Wayward Wind'. 1963 was the year the rest of the country discovered what the people of Liverpool had known for some time, that the Beatles were simply the greatest group the world has ever seen.

This was the time that Brian had been waiting and hoping and planning for. The Beatles worked incredibly hard as Brian put them through 12 months of the toughest and most punishing schedule of concert tours, one-night appearances, recording sessions, radio recordings, television appearances, photograph sessions and Press interviews. The Beatles did everything that was asked of them and Brian asked an awful lot.

They obeyed Brian's rules about behaviour to the letter. Well, almost. The boys always liked a drink as they performed and alcohol was banned at Granada cinemas where many of the concerts were held. They got round this by taking in Coca Cola which had already been heavily laced with whisky. I'd never heard of scotch and Coke before I met the boys, so to me it always seemed like a Beatles' invention.

But with a record at the top of the charts they knew this was the moment they had been waiting for since the three of them got together as schoolboys. And Ringo knew enough to do as he was told. The boys' emergence on to the national stage did not please all of their most fervent Liverpool fans who realised early on that they would see less of their favourites in future as they moved out of the grasp of Merseyside. Local legend has it that when the news of their first number one was announced at The Cavern, it was greeted with stony silence. But there wasn't much silence in the office as interest in the boys spiralled amazingly.

Gerry and the Pacemakers, Billy J. Kramer and the Dakotas, and The Big Three started having hits as well and the whole world just went completely mad for a while. Phones rang constantly. More secretaries and assistants arrived and went as Brian struggled to stay in control. The boys were on tour with Helen Shapiro. When it began, she was the star of the show, but by the time it had finished the screams for the Beatles drowned out just about everything else.

ENJOYING THEIR FAME

In April, they released 'From Me to You' which was written by John and Paul on the coach during their Helen Shapiro tour. The first LP, *Please, Please Me*, included both sides of their first two records, as well as 'Twist and Shout' and 'A Taste of Honey'. Both single and LP shot to the top of the charts and the Beatles were booked for another exhausting tour in May, this time with Roy Orbison. At the start, Orbison topped the bill and the Beatles were all impressed by his amazing voice. But as the Beatles' popularity grew and grew, the positions were reversed, and they followed The Big O. This was right because of their fanatical following, but Roy Orbison was such a great singer that his final version of 'Pretty Woman' had the fans on their feet. The Beatles were left behind the curtain wondering how on earth they were going to follow that. But they did it every time.

They could do anything and John could do more than the others. He might have left a lasting image as an anarchic rebel but I can remember clearly how excited he was when the Beatles were asked to appear on the *Morecambe and Wise* show.

I did have a scare at the *NME* Awards night when the Shadows were announced, at which the Beatles all leaped up and cheered and I was scared they were going to start taking the mickey. But they were serious. They would not have crossed the road to listen to Cliff Richard but they wanted to see the Shadows in action because they had always admired their musicianship. 'You see, Al, we're not taking the piss all the time,' said John. They just stood at the side of the stage watching in appreciation.

The boys enjoyed their fame. In those days, Brian was always keen that they should know whenever a Beatles record was going to be played on the radio. I'd pass on the information and they would stop the car, or whatever they were doing, to listen. The Beatles would have special celebration dinners for every number one. Brian loved to reward them for doing well. And as the money poured in, they started to eat a lot better as well. In that first couple of years of success, they all steadily put on a little weight. They say a true Beatles fanatic can tell from a photograph just when in that period it was taken!

These were the most amazing times for the Beatles because the public discovered them before the newspapers. There were massive crowds everywhere they performed and riots to get near them became a constant problem for the boys. George unwisely mentioned that he liked jelly babies and the fans hurled millions of the sweets at them whenever they could.

MAKING NEWS

There was a real closeness between the boys in those heady early days. They felt like they were taking on the whole world and all they needed was each other. They had their own private language and a sense of humour that was all their own. If anyone was being boring in the dressing room, the Beatles had a code for getting rid of them. They would just catch roadie Mal Evans' eye and yawn in the appropriate direction and the bore would be swiftly steered towards the exit.

But the national Press remained largely uninterested for a long time. Maureen Cleave of the London *Evening Standard*

A HINT OF BLUES

British journalist David Rowley believes that part of the appeal of "Love Me Do" can be attributed to its blues feel. Despite being adulterated by producer George Martin, the blues styling of "Love Me Do" was clear enough to be recognized by other English bands who were experimenting with that American genre in the early sixties.

'Love Me Do' had been often played live by the Beatles and their faith in it was due to the positive response it received from audiences, something George Martin had not yet witnessed. Simple in melody and lyric, its strength was an expressive blues feel that had been lost at their nervy audition in June. John, later speaking in support of it, described it as 'funky', which suggests at least that the Beatles never did justice to it on record.

Numerous unsigned bands playing live in small UK clubs in the early 1960s were playing this same imitation of soul and R&B music, which valued a song's 'feel' more than its structure. The big, conservative London-based record labels were at first resistant to this trend, though as Parlophone showed it was only a matter of time before one of them proved its commercial potential. Tellingly, Keith Richards of the Rolling Stones said that on first hearing 'Love Me Do' he felt 'sick' that another band had made this breakthrough first. The Rolling Stones, then still unsigned, were causing a small sensation as a regular live act in and around London.

David Rowley, *Beatles for Sale: The Musical Secrets of the Greatest Rock 'n' Roll Band of All Time*. London: Mainstream, 2002.

had done one of the earliest London interviews in February when she marvelled at their humour and freshness and described their famous fringes as a French hairstyle. Brian was desperate to get more national paper coverage but it didn't really arrive in a big way until the autumn. It was completely the other way round from today when tedious, talentless unknowns are hyped into the charts by carefully orchestrated Press, TV and radio campaigns. The Beatles had to earn their amazing national following the hard way.

But when it came to performing or recording, they were fantastic. They recorded their first album, *Please, Please Me*, in one remarkable 12-hour session at Abbey Road. George Martin was trying to capture live the sort of excitement the Beatles generated in their live performances in Liverpool or Hamburg. That album is still one of my favourites and I'm always amazed that John's throat holds out for the final raucous rendition of 'Twist and Shout'. John said that last effort almost killed him and his throat took months to recover. He drank pints and pints of milk because he thought it would help. In the end, they were happy with the result and it still sounds great to me today. Paul loved working at Abbey Road so much it was one of the reasons he bought a house round the corner in Cavendish Avenue.

LENNON'S HOLIDAY

One story the Press certainly didn't get at the time was that in April, in the middle of the euphoria that followed all the early success and acclaim, Brian and John went off to Spain for a holiday. So much invention and rubbish has been made of this trip by so many people since, that the truth deserves at least a brief mention. The most sensational version, of course, is that the holiday was a chance for Brian to consummate his overwhelming passion for John, which inspired him to sign the group in the first place. I'm afraid it wasn't like that.

John roared with laughter at the rumours that began afterwards. Typically, he encouraged the stories that he and Brian were gay lovers because he thought it was funny and John was one of the world's great wind-up merchants. He told me afterwards in one of our frankest heart-to-hearts that Brian never seriously did proposition him. He had teased Brian about the young men he kept gazing at and the odd ones who had found their way to his room. Brian had joked to John about the women who hurled themselves at him. 'If he'd asked me, I probably would have done anything he wanted. I was so much in awe of Brian then I'd have tried a night of vice-versa. But he never wanted me like that. Sure, I took the mickey a bit and pretended to lead him on. But we both knew we were joking. He wanted a pal he could have a laugh with and someone he could teach about life. I thought his bum boys were creeps and Brian knew that. Even completely out of my head, I couldn't shag a bloke. And I certainly couldn't lie there and let one shag me. Even a nice guy like Brian. To be honest, the thought of it turns me over.'

All the same, John was very selfish to have gone off on holiday with Brian then because it was just after Cynthia had given birth to his son Julian. John's whole romance and marriage to Cynthia was kept a secret at the time because Brian feared the effect of publicity about one of the Beatles having a wife, let alone a family.

The Beatles were on tour in April 1963 when Cynthia went into labour in Liverpool's Sefton General Hospital and it was a week before John even went to see Julian. John used to ring [his aunt] Mimi every night for reports on the baby and Brian had arranged a private room for Cynthia for a remarkable 25s a day. John tried to disguise himself to avoid publicity when he eventually went to see his wife and son and Cynthia laughed at him when she saw the fake moustache, hat and dark glasses. But it was still a wonderful moment for her as John rushed into her room and told her how clever she was. His first question was, 'Who does he look like?'

Julian had suffered from jaundice when he was born but the yellow colour had subsided by then. John took Julian in his arms and said, 'He's bloody marvellous, Cyn, isn't he absolutely fantastic?'

But even this intimate family moment was interrupted because the private room had a window on to the main ward and one of the mothers shouted, 'It's him. One of the Beatles.' John's cover was blown and he told Cyn he would have to go to avoid a fuss. He just had time to tell her that he wanted Brian to be the baby's godfather and he and Brian were taking a holiday in Spain at the end of an exhausting tour.

Cynthia told me afterwards that she was very shocked by this whole experience. Her most personal moment with her husband and their new baby had been hijacked by fans screaming at them through the window, and John had reacted by running off on holiday with his manager. Cyn knew perfectly well that John didn't have a homosexual inclination in his body, but she still didn't like being left quite literally holding the baby. But when she questioned her husband's holiday plans, John snorted, 'Being selfish again, aren't you? I've been working my ass off for months on one-night stands. Those people staring from the other side of the glass are bloody everywhere, haunting me. I deserve a holiday. And, anyway, Brian wants me to go, and I owe it to the poor guy. Who else does he have to go away with?'

Beatlemania

Hunter Davies

In the first few months of 1963, the Beatles had two charting singles ("Love Me Do" and "Please Please Me") in Britain, and Vee Jay Records had just picked up these singles for U.S. release. Manager Brian Epstein was keen to follow up the successes with a national tour and an LP release. In February the band took on both responsibilities. The British tour kicked off early in the month; it was interrupted only briefly on February 11 for the Beatles to stop in at EMI studios to record their first album in a marathon thirteen-hour session. By February 13, the band was back out on the road. The grueling tour helped push "Please Please Me" into the number one spot on many British music charts. In March, the Beatles recorded another single ("From Me to You"/"Thank You Girl") ten days before *Please Please Me*, the first album, was released in the UK.

By July 1963, the Beatles tour was attracting sell-out crowds in various parts of Britain. In August, the band recorded and released its third single. "She Loves You"/"I'll Get You" shot to number one in the *New Musical Express* chart and stayed there for five weeks. But October was the month that the craze known as Beatlemania swept the British Isles. In his well-known and well-respected 1968 biography of the Beatles, Hunter Davies recalls how the Beatles' look, image, and music carried away the young Britons and how Beatlemania impacted everything from pop culture to politics in 1963. Davies was a journalist for the *Sunday Times* (London) when he first befriended the Beatles in 1966 and began writing his personalized history of the band.

Hunter Davies, *The Beatles*, 2nd rev. edition. New York: W.W. Norton & Company, Inc., 1996. Copyright © 1996 by Hunter Davies. All rights reserved. Reproduced by permission.

Beatlemania descended on the British Isles in October 1963, just as the Christine Keeler–Profumo scandal[1] fizzled out.

It didn't lift for three years, by which time it had spread and had covered the whole world. There was perpetual screaming and *yeh-yeh*ing for three years, one long continuous succession of hysterical teenagers of every class and color, shouting uncontrollably, not one of whom could hear what was going on for the noise of each other. Each of them emotionally, mentally, or sexually excited, foaming at the mouth, bursting into tears, hurling themselves like lemmings in the direction of the Beatles or just simply fainting.

Throughout the whole of the three years it was happening somewhere in the world. Each country witnessed the same scenes of mass emotion, scenes which had never been thought possible before and which are unlikely to be ever seen again. Writing about it now makes it all sound like fiction. It is impossible to exaggerate Beatlemania because Beatlemania was in itself an exaggeration. No words can fully describe those scenes, although every major newspaper in the world has miles of words and pictures in its clipping library, giving blow-by-blow accounts of what happened when the Beatles descended on their part of the globe.

Once it had stopped, by 1967, and everyone was either overcome by exhaustion or boredom, it was difficult to believe it had all happened. Could everyone have been so mad? It wasn't just teenagers; people of all ages and all intellects had succumbed, though perhaps not all as hysterically as the teenagers.

World leaders and famous personages, who'd often started by warning or criticizing, fell over each other to drag in references to the Beatles, to show that they were in touch, to let people see that they also knew that a phenomenon of mass communication had occurred.

Anxious Fans and Hysterical Crowds

It occurred suddenly and dramatically in Britain in October 1963 and Brian Epstein said he wasn't prepared for it.

He was prepared for success, because they were already having it. What he meant was that he wasn't prepared for hysteria.

---

1. John Profumo, Britain's secretary of war, was accused of a sexual affair with a nineteen-year-old showgirl and sometime prostitute, Christine Keeler. She was also involved at the time with a Soviet naval attache and suspected spy, Yevgeny Ivanov.

"She Loves You," which had come out at the end of August, also went to number one, following the pattern of their previous two singles. As early as June, even before it had a title, thousands of fans had already ordered the next Beatle single. The day before it was on sale, there were 500,000 advance orders for it.

By September the Beatles had reached a unique position in Britain. They had the top-selling LP record, "Please Please Me." They had the top-selling EP record, "Twist and Shout." They had the top-selling single, "She Loves You."

But it wasn't until the night of October 13, 1963, that the Beatles stopped being simply an interesting pop-music story and became front-page hard news in every national newspaper. This was the night they topped the bill at the London Palladium on a show which was televised as "Sunday Night at the London Palladium." An estimated audience of fifteen million viewers watched them that night.

Argyll Street, where the Palladium is situated . . . was besieged by fans all day long. Newspapermen started arriving once the stories of the crowds got round. The stage door was blocked by fans, mountains of presents, and piles of telegrams. Inside it was almost impossible to rehearse for the continual screams of the thousands of fans chanting outside in the streets.

Other TV companies turned up, from the news departments, to record the crowd scenes, even though the show was being broadcast by a rival network. The police, taken completely by surprise, were unable to control most of the crowd. It was decided that the Beatles' getaway car should be stationed at the front doors, as everyone expected them to leave afterward by the stage door. Their car by this time was a chauffeur-driven Austin Princess. Neil's old van had long since been discarded once the hit records started appearing.

The police, thinking they were clever, moved the car slightly away from the front door, trying to conceal it. Which meant that when the Beatles did appear, shepherded by Neil [Aspinall, their road manager], they had to search wildly for the car, then make a dash of fifty yards, almost being killed by the mobs in the process.

The front page of every newspaper next day had long news stories and large pictures of the hysterical crowd scenes. The stories weren't about how well or how badly the group had played their songs, but simply about the chaos they had caused.

SOUGHT-AFTER CELEBRITIES

"From that day on," says Tony Barrow, the press officer, "everything changed. My job was never the same again. From spending six months ringing up newspapers and getting no, I now had every national reporter and feature writer chasing *me*." His job from then on became to select, along with Brian and other press officers who were later used, journalists who were allowed to interview the Beatles. They never had to ask anyone again to do anything. His job, as far as the Beatles were concerned, was simply to become an information officer. The Queen's so-called press officer is in effect an information officer. He never rings people. He is there to answer questions, or in most cases, not answer questions. The Beatles' press officers—there was eventually one who went on tour and one, Tony Barrow, in London—from then on assumed the same sort of functions.

"Even before that, I'd never been in any sense a publicist, the way most groups have publicists, thinking up publicity stunts. I didn't know about that, as I'd never been one. Brian anyway would have been against any stunts. We never used any and we never had to."

The following Wednesday Bernard Delfont announced the names for what is looked upon by most British show-business people as the biggest show of the year—the Royal Variety Performance, "That was an even greater honor than the Palladium," said Brian.

Brian might have thought so, being naturally impressed by them appearing before Royalty, but the Beatles themselves, not being nature's royalists, were more impressed by the bill—Marlene Dietrich and Maurice Chevalier.

The Beatles were back on tour when this news broke. They were still doing tour after tour and still in some cases doing ballroom dates. They were actually in Liverpool, about to appear at a Southport ballroom, when the news came out. All the national newspapers sent reporters and photographers across from their Manchester offices to get the Beatles' reactions to the news. They were obviously hoping for some satirical remarks about the Royal Family, but to Brian's relief, there were none. The Royal Variety Show was planned for November 4. Before that they continued touring in Britain and for the first time abroad, to Sweden.

In Britain each one-night stand resulted in the same hysterical crowd scenes. Everyday the newspaper had almost word-for-word the same front-page news stories, only the name of the town was different.

RIOTS AT HOME AND ABROAD

Even in smallish towns, like Carlisle, where earlier in the year they'd had trouble at a local hotel, the crowds were huge. On the night of October 24, over 600 teenagers waited all night long in Warwick Road, Carlisle, as they queued to buy tickets the next day at the ABC Cinema, where the Beatles were to appear. Most of them brought sleeping bags and slept. Some had been there for as long as thirty-six hours. When the box office opened and the line moved forward, shop windows were smashed and nine people were taken to the hospital. In bigger towns like Newcastle and Leicester the all-night queues were bigger, 4000 and 3000 respectively.

The Swedish tour, their first foreign trip since Hamburg, was a direct result of their records' sales. "She Loves You" soon reached the million figure in Britain, for which it got a gold disk, but it was also selling well in Europe, which British pop stars' records had rarely done before.

The Swedish tour lasted only five days, from the twenty-fourth of October to the twenty-ninth. This tour, day by day, made the British papers at home as well as the Swedish press and television. At a concert in Stockholm, forty policemen, with batons at the ready, stood guarding the stage to stop fans climbing on. Outside there were more police with police dogs, trying to control the fans who couldn't get in. The fans did eventually break through the barrier of police and get onto the stage. George was knocked over, but the police managed to restore order before he was trodden on.

Swedish fans were already affecting Beatle hairstyles and clothes, as British fans had also started to do. In Sweden the hairstyle was known as the Hamlet style. The Beatles themselves date the beginning of Beatlemania from a week or so later than Tony Barrow first put it. They first realized their massive popularity on October thirty-first, when they arrived back at London Airport from Sweden.

They had of course been aware of the chaos at the London Palladium two weeks previously, and all the other riots up and down the country. But this had been going on, building up all the time but less publicized, since their Cavern days. They had gotten into a pattern on tour of having to be smuggled in and out of theaters. They were trying to escape it, rather than face up to it and risk being killed.

But when they arrived back at London Airport their popularity suddenly hit them. It was their first triumphal arrival from anywhere since the Cavern welcome-homes. Thousands of screaming fans had been choking London Airport for hours. In the chaos of surrounding their arrival the car containing the Prime Minister, Sir Alec Douglas-Home, was held up. Miss World, who was also passing through London Airport at the time, was completely ignored. The airport scenes became familiar pictures for the next three years.

PERFORMING FOR ROYALTY

The Royal Variety Performance, on November 4, was held at the Prince of Wales' Theatre. The audience wasn't as big as the Palladium show but in theory much more select as the seats were about four times the normal price. It was a charity show, full of show-business establishment, minor society and rag-trade moguls, all hoping for a glimpse of the Royals. On this occasion they were the Queen Mother, Princess Margaret, and Lord Snowdon. It's said to be a difficult audience to play to. There is the nauseating tradition of the audience craning to see what effect each act is having in the royal box before they also clap or laugh.

Paul got a laugh all round from the beginning. The Beatles came on immediately after Sophie Tucker. Paul said how pleased they were to be following their favorite American group. Musically, they did their usual act—causing hysterics just by announcing they were going to sing "She Loves You." Then they did "Till There Was You" and "Twist and Shout."

For one number John asked the audience to clap their hands in time. Nodding toward the royal box, he added: "Those upstairs, just rattle your jewelry."

This joke was on every front page the next day, everyone loving the implied, though very slight, joke at the Royals' expense. All completely harmless, of course. But it was looked upon as being rather cheeky, though of course lovable, because the Beatles had become so lovable. It led the way in later years for other comedians and comperes to try to get in their Royal joke.

The Queen Mother, in talking to them afterward, showed

that she was well aware of what they did. She even made her own joky remark, though it probably wasn't meant to be joky. She asked them where they were appearing next and they said Slough. "Oh," said the Queen Mother, "that's near us."

The show was televised the following Sunday and had an audience of twenty-six million. The front-page stories about Beatles' concerts became monotonously the same. Even papers like the *Daily Telegraph*, which up to then had considered itself too staid to cover pop stories (they now religiously publish the top ten each week) gave columns to every riot. For a long time, however, they still referred in their reports, as in one about a Newcastle concert on October 28, to "teenagers fighting to get tickets for the Beatles 'pop' group. . . ." They still felt it necessary to explain who the Beatles were.

There were questions in Parliament about the thousands of extra policemen all around the country who were being made to do extra, and dangerous, duty because of the Beatles. One MP [member of Parliament] suggested that the police should withdraw and see what happened. Luckily, no one took that suggestion seriously. On November the first they began another tour, this time billed simply as the Beatles Show. There was no other joint star, as there had been with Roy Orbison, because none was needed.

In the program for this show, which toured until December 13, there were several advertisements for Beatle products. A firm in Peckham was offering Beatles Sweaters "designed specially for Beatle people by a leading British manufacturer with a top quality two-tone Beatle badge." All for 35 shillings each.

EXPLAINING THE HYSTERIA

Manufacturers all over the country were by this time competing to get a concession to use the word *Beatle* on their products. Beatles jackets—the collarless ones, usually in corduroy, first worn by Stu in Hamburg—were on sale everywhere as early as September 1963.

Beatle wigs started appearing. A factory in Bethnal Green was working night and day to keep up with the demand. It had orders from Eton College and from Buckingham Palace. Most teenage boys were growing their own Beatle-length hair. From November on there was a continuous stream of newspaper stories about schoolboys being sent home from school because of their long hair and of apprentices not being allowed into factories.

The *Daily Telegraph*, on November second, produced the first leader criticizing the Beatles hysteria. It said the mass hysteria was simply filling empty heads, just as Hitler had done. The *Daily Mirror* jumped to the Beatles' defense. "You have to be a real sour square not to love the nutty, noisy, happy handsome Beatles." The paper complimented the Beatles for not relying "on off-color jokes about homos for their fun."

They were attacked and then defended in the Church Assembly, the annual meeting of leaders of the Church of England. One bishop said they were a "psychopathetic group" and that one week of their wages could build a cathedral in Africa. But another speaker said he was a fan and that it was all healthy fun.

The *Daily Mirror* was about the first paper to drag out a tame psychologist to try to explain what was happening, a practice which kept tame psychologists all over the world, most of all in America, in easy money for the next three years. This psychologist said the Beatles were "relieving a sexual urge." Doctors later testified to say that girls had had orgasms during their concerts.

In Plymouth, on November 14, hoses had to be turned on screaming fans to control them. There was greater panic at Portsmouth because Paul had slight flu and the group had to miss a concert. Every paper gave hour-by-hour bulletins on his condition. In Birmingham on November 11 they managed to escape the crowds disguised as policemen. On November 18 a Church of England vicar got a lot of space in the papers when he asked the Beatles to tape him "Oh Come All Ye Faithful, Yeh, Yeh," for Christmas.

CONTINUING SUCCESS

EMI sales were shooting up. When the story came out about Decca and all the other companies having turned them down it was compared with 20th Century-Fox turning down *Gone with the Wind.*

At the end of November they brought out their fifth single, "I Want to Hold Your Hand." This went direct to number one. It had advance orders in Britain of one million. Their second LP came out a few days before, *With the Beatles.* This had the stark but very arty photograph on the cover showing their four heads and shoulders, dressed in black turtleneck sweaters. Their faces were cleverly lit so that one side was in the shade, as Astrid [Kirchherr, a German photographer who married Stu Sutcliffe] had done in Hamburg. When this LP was announced, at the beginning of November, it had immediate advance orders of 250,000. It was noted at the time that this was the best advance for an LP record anywhere in the world. The best Elvis Presley had done was 200,000 for his "Blue Hawaii" album.

Every big bylined feature writer was competing for an interview, waiting for hours and hours outside their dressing room, hoping for a word. Donald Zec of the *Daily Mirror* was one of the first to do a large interview with them, right at the beginning of their nationally famous days, on September 10. In describing their hairstyle, which journalists still felt they had to do, he said it was a Stone-Age cut.

By December 1963, the staid Sunday papers had got in on the act, doing long and very solemn investigations of the phenomenon, also dragging out their own psychologists, but using even longer words. The *Observer* used a picture of a guitar-shaped Cycladic fertility goddess from Amorgos that it said "dates the potency of the guitar as a sex symbol to about 4,800 years before the Beatle era." The *Sunday Times* commented on how they had enlarged the English language, bringing Liverpool words like *gear* (meaning good or great) into general usage. This rather put the Conservative politician Edward Heath in his place. Earlier he had criticized the Beatles by saying their language was "unrecognizable as the Queen's English." But Mr. Heath redeemed himself slightly later when he was reported as asking "who could have forecast only a year ago that the Beatles would prove the salvation of the corduroy industry?"

Even the *Daily Worker*, the British Communist Party newspaper, was getting its comment in. "The Mersey Sound is the voice of 80,000 crumbling houses and 30,000 people on the dole."

A GROWING BUSINESS INTEREST

By early December seven of their records, singles as well as EPs, were in the Top Twenty. On December 11 they went on the TV program *Juke Box Jury*, the four of them taking over the complete jury, and gave the show the highest rating it had ever had.

A film deal was announced. Walter Shenson and George

Ornstein, in association with United Artists, said they were going to star the Beatles in their first film, with a script by the Liverpool playwright Alun Owen. Brian Epstein was in on this deal, making sure that the Beatles were to take a large percentage. He was by now doing the same with their tours, once it was obvious that their name alone was enough to guarantee a full house everywhere. The Beatles Tour, which had begun in November, this time was "presented by Arthur Howes, by arrangement with Brian Epstein." Brian was making sure they were being involved in all the enormous profits which were being made and were putting aside their share of it each time.

In October Brian had moved his own office to London, joining Tony Barrow and the growing number of secretaries and assistants.

The fan club was also growing to huge proportions and was completely unable to cope with the thousands of application forms pouring in. There were many stories in the newspapers about poor fans not having their letters answered for months, but the deluge was just too much. By the end of the year the official fan club had almost eighty thousand paid-up members, compared with a couple of thousand at the beginning of the year.

BBC TV, like all other media, desperate for any sort of Beatle story, even when the Beatles themselves wouldn't be interviewed, did a half show from the Northern Area convention of the Beatles Fan Club from the Liverpool Empire.

At Christmastime the Beatles did a Christmas show, along with other Brian Epstein artists—Cilla Black, Billy J. Kramer, Tommy Quickly, and the Fourmost. It opened in Bradford, then Liverpool, then came to London at the Finsbury Park Empire, which was where Mal lost John's favorite guitar. The intellectual following was now in full cry. The prestigious papers were giving the group as much space as the tabloids. Paul and John were commissioned to write the music for a ballet, *Mods and Rockers.*

Brian worried at first about his own name and personality becoming famous, but eventually he couldn't help it. He realized that it made things easier for him to get things done if he was known by name almost as much as the Beatles.

"What I was worried about was all of us becoming over exposed. At first sight the endless discussion in the newspapers of the Beatles' habits, clothes, and views was exciting.

They liked it at first and so did I. It was good for business. But finally it became an anxiety. How much could they maintain public interest without rationing either personal appearances or newspaper coverage? By a stringent watch on their bookings and press contacts we just averted saturation point. But it was very close. Other artists have been destroyed by this very thing."

PUTTING-ON THE PRESS

At the time, judging by the newspaper and TV reports, it looked as though there was no control at all. Every paper every day had something on them. In one week five national newspapers were serializing their life story, most of it taken from the old handouts. Everyone remotely connected with the Beatles got himself into the newspaper. Almost anyone with any opinion on them, for or against, was guaranteed to be reported. Several papers said that Brian Epstein was the Svengali. He'd cleverly created and promoted them. Brian always denied this.

"In all our handouts," says Tony Barrow, "and in all our press dealings. Brian only stressed what was good about them. He never created any nonexistent good points.

"The Beatles were four local lads from down the street, the sort you might have seen at the local church hall. This was the essence of their personal communication with the public. This was the appeal. People identified with them from the beginning. Brian realized this and never tried to hide it."

But Brian did of course create a smooth machinery, organized their lives meticulously, never let people down—which they had always done when they were on their own. But the big attraction was the Beatles themselves. Every reporter knew that every interview would be different and funny. Ringo turned out to be just as funny as the rest of them. He was asked why he had so many rings on his fingers. He said it was because he couldn't get them all through his nose.

John, today, says they were really putting-on the press. He despised many newspapers because for long, he says, they had refused to accept them as anything more than ordinary.

"We were funny at press conferences because it was all a joke. They'd ask joke questions so you'd give joke answers. But we weren't really funny at all. It was just fifth-form humor, the sort of you laugh at at school. They were putrid. If there were any good questions, about our music, we took them seriously. Our image was only a teeny part of us. It was created by the press and by us. It had to be wrong because you can't put over how you really are. Newspapers always get things wrong. Even when bits were true it was always old. New images would catch on just as we were leaving them."

THE WORLD'S TOP GROUP

In just twelve months from the release of the first record, they had become an established part of the British way of life. Dora Bryan did a record about them at Christmas 1963, "All I Want for Christmas Is a Beatle." That even got into the hit parade. There was by now nobody else on the hit parade scene, unless you counted the other Liverpool groups, all of whom Brian Epstein managed and all of whom were being recorded by George Martin.

In 1963, out of the fifty-two weeks in the year a record produced by George Martin was at the top of the British Hit Parade for thirty-seven weeks. This is an achievement no one has ever equaled, or is likely to.

The *New Musical Express*, in its end-of-the-year charts, made the Beatles the world's top group. They polled 14,666 votes. The American group, the Everly Brothers, was runner-up with 3,232 votes. In the "British Vocal Section," the section they had been near the bottom of the year before, they polled 18,623 votes. The second group, the Searchers, were miles away with only 2,169 votes. The two highest-selling singles of the year were "She Loves You" with 1.3 million and "I Want to Hold Your Hand" with 1.25 million. Cliff Richard with "Bachelor Boy" was a long way down in third place.

The *Times* musical critic, William Mann, did a long and serious review of their music in which he said John Lennon and Paul McCartney were "the outstanding English composers of 1963."

"I think I'll invite them down for the weekend, just to see what kind of fellas they are," said Viscount Montgomery.

On December 29 in the *Sunday Times*, Richard Buckle, in reviewing John and Paul's music for the ballet *Mods and Rockers*, said they were "the greatest composers since Beethoven."

Conquering America

Philip Norman

On February 7, 1964, Pan American Flight 101 taxied along a runway at John F. Kennedy Airport in New York. Flanking the plane's path were hordes of frenzied teenagers—screaming, sobbing, and waving. Aboard Flight 101, the four Beatles assumed the crowds had assembled for some arriving dignitary, such as the president of the United States. Only when the band members exited the plane did they see banners welcoming the Beatles to America. After a short press conference at the airport, the Beatles were whisked away by limousine to the Plaza Hotel, where another five thousand fans surrounded the building. The images of the crowds at both the airport and the hotel have become symbols of Beatlemania in the United States, but they were only hint of the hysteria to come.

In the following selection from his book *Shout!: The Beatles in Their Generation*, novelist and biographer Philip Norman describes how America was ready for "a new idol, a new toy, a painkilling drug and a laugh." The Beatles' arrival had satisfied those needs. Their quick wit shined in various interviews, and their personal magnetism and musicianship charmed 23 million viewers of the February 9 episode of the Ed Sullivan variety show. The youthful craze for the band and the thousands of Beatle products reached a fever pitch after that broadcast and a subsequent appearance in Miami on February 16. Throughout the entire U.S. tour, the band was hounded by the press and barricaded in hotels by mobs of young screaming teenagers. On February 22, they returned to London, where they suffered under the same type of siege, though this time staged by loyal English fans.

Philip Norman, *Shout!: The Beatles in Their Generation.* New York: MJF Books, 1981.

On the first floor of the main terminal [of Kennedy Airport], where two hundred journalists waited, [Beatles' press officer] Brian Sommerville began to show his quarterdeck irascibility. The photographers, massed in front of reporters and TV crews, were making too much noise for any formal question to be heard. Sommerville, after several more or less polite injunctions, grabbed a microphone and snapped: "Shut up—just shut up." The Beatles concurred, "Yeah, shurrup." This produced spontaneous applause.

The New York press, with a few exceptions, succumbed as quickly as the fans. Within minutes, one svelte and sarcastic woman journalist was babbling into a telephone: "They are absolutely too cute for words. America is going to just *love* them." On another line, an agency reporter began his dispatch: "Not since MacArthur returned from Korea. . . ." Meanwhile, in the conference room, their one hundred and ninety-eight colleagues continued the interrogation which was supposed to have been ironic and discomfiting but which had produced anything but discomfiture. The Beatles were at their flash-quick, knockabout, impudent best.

"Are you going to have a haircut while you're in America?"

"We had one yesterday," John replied.

"Will you sing something for us?"

"We need money first," John said.

"What's your secret?"

"If we knew that," George said, "we'd each form a group and manage it."

"Was your family in show business?" John was asked.

"Well, me Dad used to say me Mother was a great performer."

"Are you part of a teenage rebellion against the older generation?"

"It's a dirty lie."

"What do you think of the campaign in Detroit to stamp out the Beatles?"

"We've got a campaign of our own," Paul said, "to stamp out Detroit."

Outside the terminal, four chauffeur-driven Cadillacs waited. The Beatles, ejected rather than emerging from the rear entrance, were each lifted bodily by two policemen and thrust into a Cadillac. Long after they had returned to England, their arms would still bear the marks of this helpful assistance. Paul, in addition, had a handful of his hair wrenched by a photographer, to see if it was a wig. "Get out of here, buddy," a policeman told the leading chauffeur, "if you want to get out alive."

AT THE PLAZA HOTEL

Outside the stately Plaza Hotel, facing Central Park, the fountains were engulfed by a shrieking mob, against which a squad of mounted policemen bounced ineffectually like corks. Reservations at the Plaza had been made a month earlier in the individual names of Lennon, McCartney, Harrison and Starr, four London "businessmen." At the time, the hotel checked only as far as to ascertain their "good financial status." As soon as the true nature of their business became known, a Plaza representative went on radio, offering them to any other New York hotel that would take them.

As the four Cadillacs sped in from Kennedy, set among their weaving and shouting and grimacing motorcade, the Plaza strove not to capitulate. The Palm Court served tea, as usual, with violin music, though the orchestra leader was vexed to receive requests for Beatles songs. Waiters moved among the pillars and heaped pastries, discreetly requesting the odd errant guest to remove his Beatle wig.

The Beatles and their party had been allocated the hotel's entire twelfth floor. A special force from the Burns Detective Agency was on duty around the clock, to screen all arrivals and conduct periodic searches in the floors above, where some girls had climbed several hundred fire stairs to lie in wait. A bevy of under-managers ran around, fearful, as well they might be, for the hotel's cherished fabric. When a photographer asked John Lennon to lie down on a bed and show his boots, a Plaza man interrupted, "Oh, no—*that's* not the image we want to project." "Don't worry," John told him. "We'll buy the bed."

Interconnecting suites, ten rooms in all, had been provided for the Beatles, their solitary wife, their two autograph-manufacturing road managers and their overworked publicist. Only Brian had separate accommodations, on the Central Park side, far from everyone else.

Already, visitors were arriving, or trying to arrive. One of the first to get through the security was Geoffrey Ellis, Brian's old Liverpool friend, the Royal Insurance man. "The whole scene was extremely surrealistic," Ellis says. "The Beatles were all sitting round with transistor radios in their ears, listening to their records playing and watching themselves on television at the same time."

All the evening TV news bulletins carried the Kennedy Airport scenes as the top story, though not all expressed unqualified delight. On NBC, Chet Huntley, the celebrated front man, quivered with bilious distaste. "Like a good little news organization, we sent three cameramen out to Kennedy this afternoon to cover the arrival of a group from England, known as the Beatles. However, after surveying the film our men returned with, and the subject of that film, I feel there is absolutely no need to show any of that film." A dissident radio station, WNEW, kept saying that "I Want to Hold Your Hand" made some people want to hold their noses.

On every other pop frequency, Beatle voices could be heard, conversing in prerecorded form or as they had spoken a few minutes earlier, live from their hotel suite. Fast-talking disc jockeys found them an easy target, instantly friendly and funny and willing to endorse anything or anyone. The great success in this field was scored by "Murray the K" Kaufman of station WINS; having first interviewed the Beatles by telephone, he arrived in their suite, accompanied by an all-girl singing group, and was seldom, if ever, absent thereafter. . . .

THROUGH THE FIRST NIGHT

Shortly after their arrival, George Harrison went to bed, complaining of a sore throat. He had been unwell in Paris, too, dictating his *Daily Express* column—as he was to continue to do—without mention of the disconcerting French habit of administering medicines in suppository form. His elder sister, Louise, who had just arrived from St. Louis, moved into the Plaza to nurse him.

The other three, despite the crowds outside, managed some limited after-dark movement. Paul visited the Playboy Club, leaving subsequently with a bunny girl. The Lennons and Ringo, under Murray the K's garrulous protection, went to the Peppermint Lounge, finding it the home of the Twist no longer; its resident group were imitation Beatles. Later, John and Cynthia scuttled back past the photographers, their two heads covered by a coat. Ringo did not return: it was feared for a time that he might have been kidnapped. He returned in the early hours, unaware of the frenzied unease he had caused.

The next morning, it drizzled. Twelve floors below, the crowds and police horses still struggled together in a muted chant of "She Loves You." Brian, in his sequestered drawing room, made a series of urgent telephone calls. The first was to Walter Hofer, the attorney, on West 57th Street. Hofer, at this time, was not sure if he was still NEMS' New York lawyer. "Brian told me, 'You're our attorney—we need you over here.' He gave me the job of dealing with all the Beatles' fan mail. I put my usual messenger service to work on it. Later on, I got this call from the messenger. 'Mister—I'm seventy-seven years old! There's thirty-seven sacks of mail here.'

"We set up a special department in another hotel to deal with it. One of the letters that was opened had come from Lyndon B. Johnson. Another was from the manager of the Plaza. 'When are you guys going to settle your check?' it said.". . .

ON ED SULLIVAN'S SHOW

At the Ed Sullivan Theatre on West 53rd Street, a set had been constructed of half a dozen inward-pointing white arrows. The program designer explained to a posse of journalists his desire "to symbolize the fact that the Beatles are *here.*" Even for the rehearsal, with [Beatles' road manager] Neil Aspinall standing in for George, three high-ranking CBS executives were turned away at the door. Sullivan himself was all amiability, rebuking his musical director for having told *The New York Times* the Beatles would last no longer than a year, and threatening to put on a Beatle wig himself if George was not well enough for the transmission. He became a little less amiable when Brian Epstein approached him and said grandly: "I would like to know the exact wording of your introduction." "I would like you to get lost," Ed Sullivan replied.

The "Sullivan Show" on February 9 was watched by an audience of seventy million, or sixty percent of all American television viewers. At the beginning, a congratulatory telegram was read out from Elvis Presley. Conditioned as they were to hyper-unreality, this event still gave pause to Liverpool boys who had listened to "Houn' Dog" under the bedcovers, and struggled to learn the words of "All Shook Up" as it was beamed from its inconceivable Heaven.

The image carried across America bore helpful subtitles giving each Beatle's name. John Lennon's subtitle added: "Sorry, girls—he's married."

The *New York Herald-Tribune*, next morning, called them "seventy-five percent publicity, twenty percent haircut and five percent lilting lament." *The Washington Post* called them "asexual and homely." *The New York Times* carried reviews by both the television and the music critic. The former judged the Beatles "a fine mass placebo" while the latter, anxious to out-obfuscate William Mann, discovered in "All My Loving" "a false modal frame . . . momentarily suggesting the mixolydian mode. . . ." Earl Wilson, the *New York Post* columnist, was photographed at the head of his afternoon's paragraphs in a bald wig. From UPI came the news that Billy Graham, the evangelist, had broken a lifetime's rule by watching television on the Sabbath.

On that one night, America's crime rate was lower than at any time during the previous half-century. Police precinct houses throughout New York could testify to the sudden drop in juvenile offenses. In all the five boroughs, not one single car hubcap was reported stolen.

THE RIGHT MOMENT

The nervous plans, the small-scale hopes, the little deals for cut-price fees, all coalesced in a moment that was miraculously right. America, three months earlier, had been struck dumb by a great and terrible event [when John F. Kennedy was assassinated]. America now found her voice again through an event which no psychiatrist could have made more therapeutically trivial. That voice was in itself therapeutic, reassuring a suddenly uncertain people that, at least, they had not lost their old talent for excess.

It was a moment when the potential existed for a madness which nothing indigenously American could unleash. It was a moment when all America's deep envy of Europe, and the eccentricity permitted to older-established nations, crystalized in four figures whose hair and clothes, to American eyes, placed them somewhere near Shakespeare's *Hamlet*. It was a moment simultaneously gratifying America's need for a new idol, a new toy, a painkilling drug and a laugh.

On the morning after the "Ed Sullivan Show," the Beatles were brought to the Plaza Hotel's Baroque Room to give a press conference that was itself record-breaking, both in size and fatuousness. Even superior organs like *Time* magazine and *The New Yorker* stiffened themselves to the task of determining whether Beatle hair was correctly described as "bangs" and their footwear as "pixie boots." *The Saturday Evening Post* had sent a photographer with $100,000-worth of equipment to shoot a cover. The *New York Journal-American* had sent Dr. Joyce Brothers, a psychologist with flicked-out blonde hair and her own television show. Dr. Brothers had her pulse humorously taken by the Beatles and afterwards reminded her stunned readership that "Beatles might look unappetizing and inconsequential, but naturalists have long considered them the most successful order of animals on earth."

The hideous arc-light, the poking, jostling lenses, the questions from people who still had difficulty in telling them apart, all seemed to make no impression on the Beatles' happy obligingness, their impudent deference. It was the stamina bred through Hamburg and Litherland nights, the shared wit sharpened by years of talking their way around trouble. "Either they're employing the most marvelous concealed gag man," Maureen Cleave cabled the London *Evening Standard*, "or Bob Hope should sign them up right away."

INQUISITION AND GROWING FEARS

"What do you think of the Playboy Club?" Paul was asked.

"The Playboy and I are just good friends."

"Why aren't you wearing a tie?" a woman journalist snapped at George.

"Why aren't *you* wearing a hat?"

The inquisition continued all day, without a break for lunch. Instead, some plates of hotel chicken were brought in. "I'm sorry to interrupt you while you're eating," a woman reporter said, "but what do you think you'll be doing in five years' time?"

"Still eating," John replied.

"Have you got a leading lady for your movie?"

"We're trying to get the Queen," George said. "She sells."

"When do you start rehearsing?"

"We don't," John said.

"Oh, yes, we do," Paul put in.

"We don't, Paul does," John amended. Some papers had already elicited the fact that among the other three, Paul was referred to as "the star."

The American press, in its wild scramble, paid little attention to the other young Englishman, in a polka-dotted foulard scarf, who stood at one side, observing the scene

with what *The New York Times* described as "a look of hau-
teur." Even when Jay Livingstone—the same Capitol boss
who had said, "We don't think the Beatles will do anything
in this market"—stepped beamingly forward to present
them with two million-sale Gold Discs, Brian still did not allow himself the relaxation of a smile. "He had ice water in
his veins before," another Capitol man remarked. "Now it's
turned to vinegar."

This was a mistaken diagnosis. What Brian's demeanor in
fact betrayed was a fierce desire to seem coolly imper-
turbable even as, on every side, he could feel important matters slithering from his grasp. The frequent rows he was
having with Brian Sommerville provided his only outlet for
that great, growing fear.

The record side, to begin with, was in chaos. New York
shops already had on sale discs by groups called the "Beetles" or "Bugs," in some cases illustrated by a spurious likeness, in one case, at least, innocently advertised on radio by
the *true* Beatles. Hardly less abhorrent to Brian was MGM's
release of "My Bonnie," the same record, from Hamburg
days, which had first led him to the Cavern Club. Implicit in
his dream for the Beatles was that they should disown all existence before his became entwined with theirs.

"Please Please Me," now at Number Three in the *Billboard* chart, was bringing vast profits to the hitherto obscure Vee Jay label in Chicago. Vee Jay's president, it so
chanced, was also a client of Brian's New York attorney, Walter Hofer. Vee Jay persuaded Brian to sue them as a publicity stunt, with Hofer revealed as lawyer to both parties. Capitol Records preempted this wheeze with an injunction to
stop Vee Jay issuing further Beatle records. Vee Jay, sure of
their ground, retained the law firm of ex-Vice-President Ad-
lai Stevenson. Capitol responded by engaging the Chicago
law firm of Mayor Richard Daley.

MERCHANDISING BEATLEMANIA

Only now, too, was Brian starting to realize what a cata-
strophic deal had been made on his behalf with Nicky
Byrne's Seltaeb merchandising company. In the aftermath of
the "Ed Sullivan Show," Beatle goods were pouring into the
New York shops. REMCO industries had already produced
100,000 Beatle dolls. Beatle wigs were flopping off the production line at the rate of 35,000 a day. The over-indulged

American child could choose from a range including Beatle masks, pens, bow ties, "Flip Your Wig" games, edible discs and "Beatle nut" ice cream. Agreement was reportedly pending between Seltaeb and a major cola company. Woolworth's and Penney's were negotiating to put "Beatle counters" in hundreds of their stores, coast to coast. *The Wall Street Journal* estimated that by the end of the year $50 million worth of Beatle goods would have been sold in America.

Nor was it reassuring to observe the progress around New York of the man whose company's share of the profits—$5 million at least—would be ninety percent. For Nicky Byrne did business on a magnificent scale. His lunches took place at the Four Seasons or the New York Jockey Club. His two chauffeur-driven limousines—on twenty-four-hour standby—would frequently be passed over in favor of a private helicopter. His style quickly communicated itself to the five young men from Chelsea who were his partners. Lord Peregrine Eliot has pleasant memories of dropping into the Seltaeb office, once or twice a week, to draw a $1,000 bill from petty cash.

Nicky Byrne argued—and still argues—that it was the only way to do business with large American corporations. He is equally firm on a point later to be disputed—that as the money in manufacturers' advances poured into Seltaeb, the ten percent due to Brian and the Beatles was paid over to them within seven days.

"When Brian arrived in New York, I'd just banked $97,000. So, of course, I handed a check to Brian for $9,700. He was delighted at first. 'Now,' he said, 'how much of this do I owe you?' 'Nothing, Brian,' I said. 'That's your ten percent.' He was amazed and furious all at the same time. 'But this is *marvelous*, Nicky,' he was saying—because he'd been told I'd fixed the airport business. 'How did you *do* it, Nicky—but you had no *right* to do it! But it was marvelous, Nicky.'". . .

ON TO WASHINGTON

On February 11, the Beatles were to fly to Washington to give their first American concert, at the Coliseum Sports Arena. The booking had been made for Brian by Norman Weiss, of the General Artists Corporation, to help offset the loss on the overall trip. Brian had also accepted an invitation from the British Ambassador to a function as yet unclearly defined. "Is it true," the press kept asking them, "that you're going to a masked ball?" Sir Alec Douglas Home, Britain's Prime Minister, also due in Washington for talks with President Lyndon Johnson, had wisely put his arrival back by one day.

The morning of their departure, snow began falling thickly on New York. Led by George Harrison, the Beatles flatly refused to fly in a "fookin' blizzard." They were, however, amenable to traveling by train. A private carriage was sought, and miraculously appeared in the magnificent shape of an Edwardian sleeping car from the old Richmond, Fredericksburg and Potomac Railroad. This equipage drew out of a shrieking Pennsylvania Station, carrying, with the Beatles and their entourage, dozens of journalists, several TV crews and the egregious Murray the K. Cynthia Lennon, disguised by sunglasses and a brunette wig, was almost left behind on the platform.

At Washington's Union Station, 3,000 teenagers flung themselves against the twenty-foot-high wrought-iron platform gates. Seven thousand more filled the Coliseum, an arena with the stage in the center, like a boxing ring. While the Beatles performed, Brian Sommerville had to keep running out to turn them in a different direction. The Washington fans, having read George Harrison's joke about liking jelly babies, resolutely pelted the stage with America's version, the jelly bean—often not troubling to remove them from the packet—as well as buttons, hair rollers and spent flash bulbs. A policeman near the stage philosophically screwed a .38-caliber bullet into each of his ears. And Brian Epstein, once again, was noticed standing and weeping.

The British Embassy visit had been arranged by Brian Sommerville, an old shipmate of the Naval attaché there. The Beatles agreed to go only because Brian thought it would be good for the image. Upon arriving, they were greeted by the ambassador, Sir David Ormsby-Gore, pleasantly enough. What followed was extremely unpleasant, though not atypical of Foreign Office social life. Men in stiff collars and their gin-and-tonic wives pushed and struggled for autographs, at the same time exclaiming in patrician amusement, "Can they actually *write?*" One cawing female produced nail scissors and cut off a piece of Ringo's hair. The purpose of this visit, they discovered, was to announce the prizes in an Embassy raffle. When John Lennon demurred, a group of young Foreign Office types formed threateningly around him. Ringo, touching his shoulder, said amicably, "Come on—let's get it over with."

The story, when given in the British papers, caused a major parliamentary incident. A Conservative M.P., Joan Quennell, called on the Foreign Secretary, R.A. Butler, to confirm or deny that the Beatles had been manhandled by Embassy personnel. Mr. Butler replied that, on the contrary, the Beatles' manager had written to Lady Ormsby-Gore, thanking her for a delightful evening.

At the White House, meanwhile, Sir Alec Douglas Home had arrived for his talks with President Lyndon Johnson. The big, bewildered Texan, catapulted into charge of the world's richest nation, had one thing at least in common with the tweedy, skeletal English earl. "I like your advance guard," LBJ quipped. "But don't you think they need haircuts?"

And in New York, Sid Bernstein, that portly but quick-witted promoter, sat on the staircase at Carnegie Hall, listening to an uproar which made even the framed portraits of Schubert and Ravel jig slightly on the corridor wall. His "phenomenon," mistaken by that Polish lady for a string quartet, had in one night recouped Sid Bernstein the losses suffered in promoting the 1960 Newport Jazz Festival. Celebrities like David Niven and Shirley MacLaine had begged for tickets, but had been refused. Mrs. Nelson Rockefeller, with her two daughters, had waited half an hour just for a peep into the dressing room. . . .

WITH SULLIVAN IN MIAMI

Next morning, the police barricades were removed from the front of the Plaza Hotel; its elegant lobby grew quiet but for the headlines on the newsstand counter. BRITAIN'S BOY BEATLES BUZZ BY, BOMB BOBBYSOXERS. AUDIENCE SHRIEKS, BAYS AND ULULATES. A large sum of money, which CBS had paid into the hotel for the use of the Beatles' party, was found to be untouched. Nobody even knew it was there.

The Beatles were aboard a National Airlines jet, bound for Miami and their second "Ed Sullivan Show," their course to the southwest plotted by a flight engineer in a Beatle wig. On landing, they were greeted by four "bathing beauties," a chimpanzee and a crowd of 7,000 which, in its emotion, smashed twenty-three windows and glass doors within the terminal precincts. The bathing beauties—from now on a regular but ambiguous fixture of all American journeys—each began furiously to kiss her apportioned Beatle. Police intervention was necessary to stop them from being kissed all the way to their limousines and beyond. At the Hotel

Deauville, a dimly lit Versailles turned endways into the sky above Miami Beach, each was decanted into his own lofty, luxurious, three-room prison cell. For the Deauville, like the New York Plaza, was in a state of screaming siege. Two enterprising girls had themselves wrapped in two parcels addressed to the Beatles, but were apprehended on delivery.

George Martin, their record producer, coincidentally in America, came down to Miami to see them, bringing his wife-to-be, Judy Lockhart-Smith. Martin watched the Beatles rehearse in bathing trunks in the hotel ballroom, and later repay Ed Sullivan's $3,500 with a performance destined to break every record in audience ratings for televised entertainment. So far as such things can ever be computed, seventy-five million Americans watched the "Sullivan Show" that night. During the transmission, from the hotel's Mau Mau Club, a girl next to George Martin broke off sobbing and bouncing to stare at him in surprise. "Do *you* like them, *too*, sir?" she asked.

Ed Sullivan nearly smiled. Cassius Clay [the boxer now known as Muhammad Ali] flourished Ringo Starr aloft like a talisman against Sonny Liston, against whom he was shortly to contest the world heavyweight title. Clay, a peerless siphoner of publicity, had invited the Beatles to visit him at his 5th Street gymnasium. He gave his opinion that they were the greatest but *he* was still the prettiest.

Their only escape from the crowds and press was a day spent at the beach-side mansion of a Capitol Records executive. Sergeant Buddy Bresner, a Miami cop who had befriended them, arranged for them to escape from the Deauville in the back of a butcher's truck while other policemen brought decoy guitar cases out through the front lobby.

George Martin and Judy joined them for that first real respite since they had sunbathed on the seafront at Margate. Brian was there, too, with his temporary assistant, Wendy Hanson. The householder, though absent, had left an armed bodyguard to look after them. Their protector barbecued steaks for them with a cigarette in his mouth, his shoulder holster clearly visible. "Brian was complaining about all the bootleg records that were coming out," George Martin remembers. "Suddenly, this tough-looking guy who was barbecuing our steaks leaned forward and said, 'You want we should take care of them for you, Mr. Epstein?' It was a *very* sinister moment."

The Far East Tour

Glenn A. Baker

Although the far eastern leg of the Beatles' 1964 world tour is often glossed over in favor of accounts of Beatlemania in England and the United States, the band's conquest of Australia was significant. As author Glenn A. Baker maintains, "No single instance of Beatlemania throughout the globe ever came close to the intensity and sheer magnitude of the social upheaval which accompanied the 1964 Australian Beatles' tour. No street crowds in New York, London or Liverpool ever eclipsed the antipodean hordes which, at times, comprised more than half the entire population of a city."

When the Beatles arrived in Sydney, Australia, on June 11, only three band members were present. Ringo Starr had suffered a severe case of tonsillitis while in England eight days previously. He would not join the world tour until June 14, when the band arrived in Melbourne. The Australian crowds that flocked to see the Ringo-less Beatles, however, were still impressive. In the following account, Glenn Baker describes the frenzy of Beatles fans in Adelaide on June 13. While Adelaide was normally "a bastion of Victorian decorum," both the town's elite and its screaming youth turned out, hoping to rub shoulders with or just catch a glimpse of these captivating celebrities.

Though it appeared that every upstanding citizen of Adelaide was smitten hopelessly with Beatlemania, such was not the case. Conservative educationalists, employing supression tactics that would not have been out of place on the Gulag Archipelago, managed to remove many thousands of potential welcomers from the front lines.

Adelaide Girls High School students suffered the worst. In

Glenn A. Baker, *The Beatles Down Under: The 1964 Australian and New Zealand Tour.* Buckinghamshire, UK: Magnum Imprint, 1996. Copyright © 1996 by Magnum Imprint. Reproduced by permission.

(more than twenty) letters delivered to the *News* they pointed out that, although only two streets away from the motorcade passage, they were confined to a small central yard. "I am a prisoner at Adelaide Girls High Prison," one letter read. "They barred the gates and guarded them with prefects. All that was missing was loaded rifles. Inside the school we had demonstrations and even fights. Some colleges came from the other side of town but we girls were not allowed to go 220 yards in our lunch hour. Yet we had to walk more than a mile and stand in sweltering heat for over two hours to see the Queen."

At Walford Church of England Grammer School in Unley 200 senior students staged a sit down strike when teachers confiscated their transistor radios during the arrival description. They sat on the asphalt playground chanting, "We Want The Beatles," until teachers persuaded them to return to classes. Headmistress Miss N. Morrison curtly explained to a reporter that "transistors are banned from the school."

Brighton High School students slow-clapped during assembly and inserted "yeah yeah yeah" into the school hymn. Four students from Port Adelaide Technical High School rang the Education Department three times requesting permission to see the Beatles parade. "They put the phone down in our ears the third time," said one incredulously.

Of course, not every school became an instant internment centre. Quite a few headmasters took advantage of the very obscure Arbor Day to grant their students a half day holiday (to the best of educated opinion, there is no other known instance of Australians celebrating the tree planting day in such a manner).

THE MOTORCADE

Plympton High School headmaster Mr. J.G. Goldsworthy sent circulars to parents inviting them to give written permission for their children to leave school grounds to see the Beatles and got a response of ninety-five per cent. "I have no objections at all to these four young gentlemen," he said. "The highway is only a hundred yards from the school and the procession does fall completely within the school lunchbreak." Adelaide Boys High students were allowed to line both sides of Anzac Highway and girls from Vermont Technical High School were permitted to walk a mile to the route.

Inspector Wilson of the Traffic Division criticised the lack of control of schoolchildren grouped along the highway, suggesting that teachers should have exercised more control. What he didn't realise was that far more control than was reasonable was being wielded just streets away.

From Anzac Highway, the motorcade wound through West Terrace, North Terrace and King William Street, the estimated forty-minute journey taking a little over an hour and clocking in at a mean 9 mph. From North Terrace the bursting crowds caused nightmarish headaches. Police on foot, motorbikes and horses formed a ring around the car and struggled to clear a driveable space before it. Inch by inch the beseiged vehicle moved toward the beckoning iron gates of the Town Hall.

"Outside the Town Hall, the kids were physically lifting the cars off the road," says Ernie Sigley. Adelaide is the most English city in Australia, particularly around the migrant area of Elizabeth, but it does have a reputation as 'the city of churches,' a bastion of Victorian decorum. Such an outpouring of unrestrained fervour was, therefore, all the more unbelievable. But it was happening, as newsreels, newspapers and the Beatles themselves would later attest.

Ten council employees were required to edge open the gates and allow the battered car entry. Once safe inside, the four were escorted to the Lord Mayor's chambers for their first civic reception in Australia.

At Town Hall

Out on the balcony it was as much [local disc jockey] Bob Francis' moment of glory as the Beatles'. He scurried about, back and forth, positioning each moptop and pointlessly urging the crowd of 30,000 to quieten down. With a reasonable PA set up, he was able to briefly interview each of the obviously shell-shocked Beatles. George yelled, "Hello! Hello! It's marvellous, it's fabulous, the best reception ever." Jimmy [Nicol, stand-in drummer for Ringo] got a medium response when introduced, with some booing evident. Carried away by the moment he gushed, "Oh this is the best I've ever seen anywhere in the world!" John had real difficulty putting his words together. His voice wavered emotionally as he declared, "Yes it's definitely the best we've ever been to, it's great [a huge swell of vocal approval], it's marvellous." Told there were only a million people in the State, he butted in with, "and they're all here aren't they?" For Paul, it might just as well have been another concert stage in yet another nameless city. Slickly he spruiked, "Hello everybody. How are you, alright? Thank you very much. It's marvellous . . . this is fantastic, thank you."

Inside the Town Hall, the Beatles faced ninety friends of friends. In the sombre Queen Adelaide room, normally reserved for visiting dignitaries, they spent twenty-five minutes chatting to Mayor Irwin and his wife and were presented with (still more) toy koala bears. Welcoming them, the good Mayor said, "We are delighted to have you in Adelaide and for having turned on a better day for you than they did in Sydney." Sipping orange juice and Cokes, the group responded to cries of "speech" by shoving John forward to state once more, "We are pleased to be here. It's the best welcome we've ever had."

After the Mayor had got Paul to autograph an Oliphant cartoon from the *Advertiser*, the four were smuggled out through a back entrance of the Land Titles Office into a waiting car on Flinders Street and off to the squat two-storey South Australian Hotel on North Terrace. It was twenty minutes before the street throng woke up to the deception. Meanwhile, police chiefs were beating their chests loudly. Mounted Police Inspector J.F. Crawley said it was the proudest day of his life. Deputy Commissioner Mr. G.M. Leane said, "I am proud of the way in which the police and crowds conducted themselves. It was a credit to Adelaide." Supt. Vogelesang thanked teenagers for their cooperation, and Inspector E.L. Calder, in charge of the Town Hall operations, thanked the Beatles for waving from both sides of the balcony.

INTERVIEWS

Bob Francis went to the hotel with the Beatles and for the next two days made certain he was out of their presence for as little time as possible. He had booked the suite next door to the four and a landline was installed so that he could do hourly interviews and descriptions direct to air. "I had these four large blowups of the boys," he reveals, "and if ever there wasn't enough hysteria when it was time for an on-air segment, I just stuck one of these out on the balcony and the kids went crazy enough for it to sound great on air."

At the press conference John repeated, with a little less visible emotion, "It's the best welcome we've had anywhere in the world." But didn't they say that everywhere they went?

"No, we say 'It compares very favourably with those else-where.' This is easily the best."

Told that the British police had credited them with help-ing combat juvenile delinquency, John guardedly replied, "We don't preach to anyone but we are glad to hear that we are helping the problem." Asked who had invented the chant of "yeah, yeah, yeah," he said that many other rockers, in-cluding Elvis, had been using it for years. "I forget whether Paul or I thought of using it in a song. It was six months ago, that's a long time." Quizzed about Hong Kong he revealed that he had bought [his wife] Cynthia a jade ring in the city but added, "I don't know if it's any good." He also revealed that he rang his wife almost every night but that he usually rang "at the wrong times when everybody's in bed. But Paul's rectified this problem by wearing two watches." Did he imagine that there would be kangaroos in Australian streets? "No, but I thought that there would be skyscrapers around the water and then desert inside." The conference was then wrapped up with an assurance that Ringo would be definitely arriving in Australia on Sunday morning and would be waiting for them when they reached Melbourne.

BESIEGED

Unlike other cities, where the crowds would substantially dissolve after each balcony appearance, the hordes re-mained constant outside the Southern Australia Hotel, keep-ing up a twenty-four hour chant of "We Want the Beatles." "There was no way you could get a good night's sleep." says [EMI promotions manager] Kevin Ritchie. "There was the constant noise which drove you up the wall. It was like a Chinese water torturer: There was the temptation to check out and go to another hotel across town but the worry that we might miss something kept us all at the nerve centre."

"They'd get bored," related Bob Francis, "walk out on the balcony for a wave, see the crowds, come back in and go 'Fu-uuuuuck! What is this all about?' We'd laugh, listen to John tell jokes, drink and play around but we never talked about what was outside the window. John would say, 'We're here so let's have a drink and a chat, nothing's different,' and I'm sure he meant it. George wasn't able to handle it like that, it seemed to upset him a bit."

"I found George wandering around the hotel feeling des-perately homesick just after the press conference," says

Ritchie. "He was feeling a little bit left out and a bit over-come by the welcome. He said he desperately wanted to get home." George had, it seems, had an argument of sorts with [girlfriend] Patti Boyd just before leaving England and the si-lence hurt the most when the others rang their respective lovelies each night.

But for John and Paul at least, there were the usual diver-sions to ward off homesickness. "They let the girls they wanted get to them," says Francis. "Top class models and other choice pieces. With all this at their feet their attitude was very cynical. They referred to all the girls who got to them as 'f—in' molls.' they didn't respect any of them."

Like a great many other media figures who got close to the Beatles in all parts of the world, Bob Francis suddenly had more friends than he could cope with. "People that I hadn't seen in five years would ring me up and say 'Bob, you probably don't remember me but . . . ' and ask for free tick-ets or a chance to meet the Beatles. You see, they'd bignote themselves to their friends by boasting 'Bob Francis—my best mate. He'll introduce me to the Beatles, no sweat,' and they got a very rude shock when I told them where to go . . . to buy tickets that is.

"I did take a few autograph books to Neil Aspinall to see if he could get the boys to sign then. He just looked at me con-temptuously and snarled 'Oh f— man, don't be stupid. I do all the autographs inside the hotels. They don't do any,' and then sat down and knocked them all over in a few seconds. I wasn't naive but things like that came as a great surprise back in 1964."

THE FIRST CONCERT AND BEYOND

Australia's first experience of the Beatles in concert . . . was, to put it mildly, unlike any visual spectacular staged before it. Journalists from all over Australia had flown in for the 6 P.M. and 8 P.M. shows and more than one was to be seen skulking out mid-set with a mortified visage and hands planted firmly over ears. Jimmy Nicol was in an emotional state and flayed the skins relentlessly; giving Australia something to remem-ber him by. The other three Beatles were visibly overjoyed at the uninhibited reaction of the Adelaide fans.

That night the Beatles slighted Adelaide society by failing to make an appearance at an exclusive party in the Adelaide hills, twenty miles from the city. A Viennese chef had spent more than three weeks preparing some £500 worth of exotic food and had even created two new dishes, including replicas of the four musicians carved out of boiled eggs.

Up in the hills they waited, Adelaide's elite, the four "British Dolly Birds" chosen to be Beatle companions and a vast media/industry pool, including Ernie Sigley, Bob Francis, Alec Martic, Ron Tremain and Jim Oram. But when the food began to get cold and the likelihood of an exalted presence became more remote, Chef Gelenscer declared the party "on" and the guests hungrily tucked into lobsters, hams and caviar.

Unconcerned, the Beatles were in their hotel suite with TV compere Bob Moors and a few of his [television station] ADS 7 associates, having a quiet party. "I had told them of the secret society party and they were not enthusiastic," Moors explained. "They said they wanted something more private where they could relax, not be stared at and not have to answer the usual questions. I suggested a little get together at the hotel and they agreed." Dave Lincoln [a member of the Phantoms] has a slightly different slant: "They were such regular guys that they didn't want to do a lot of things unless everybody, all the supports and workers, were invited along as well. That's why they said no to that ritzy Adelaide party."

After a midnight meal of soft boiled eggs, steaks, chicken and salad, the Beatles retired at 3 A.M. Out in the street, the faithful were jealously guarding their prime positions, ready for Saturday's balcony appearances. Younger fans began arriving at dawn, helping to increase the volume of the endless chant, "We Want the Beatles." Blissfully unaware, four fatigued Beatles slept soundly through till midday and beyond.

In other parts of the hotel, four bitterly disappointed girls were preparing to check out. They had taken two £9 rooms for the night in the hope of meeting their idols. Christine Limpus, 18 of Hectorville and Julie Williams, 16 of Wingfield made it as far as the doorway of the Beatles' suite on Friday night before being ordered back downstairs. As they left the hotel just before noon, without having seen so much as a strand of hair, Julie pouted miserably. "It isn't fair. I bet they weren't even told we were here. And I'll bet they don't know that my birthday is two days after Paul's and that we're both left handed and that we both have brown eyes and hair. I bet they don't!"

The other two hotel guests were just a little bit smarter. Seventeen-year-old Heni Timmers and sixteen-year-old Anne Aucott of Mitchell Park tarried a little and managed to collar a security guard. Apparently touched by their blubbering, he made enquiries and secured a meeting for them later in the day.

CHAPTER 3

EXPERIMENTS

THE BEATLES

The Beatles' Films and Their Impact

Bob Neaverson

On July 6, 1964, *A Hard Day's Night* premiered in London. Directed by Richard Lester and shot only ten days after the Beatles returned from America, the film successfully captured the band's wit and charm and brought the hysteria of Beatlemania to the screen. Filmed in black and white, the low-budget movie was mainly a showcase for the Beatles' music and their popularity. Both the film and its subsequent sound track were big hits with fans the world over. In Liverpool, Tony Barrow, a journalist and album sleeve note writer for Decca Records, estimated that one-quarter of the city's 750,000 inhabitants turned out for the film's debut on July 10.

In 1965, Lester returned to helm the Beatles' second film, *Help!* Instead of contending with Beatlemania, *Help!* focused on the zany fantasy life of the Beatles (though the plot actually dealt with a Hindu cult bent on retrieving a ring from Ringo's finger). Critics praised the picture, which undoubtedly benefited from Lester's stewardship. Two years later, in 1967, Paul McCartney took the reins of the Beatles' own fledgling film project. His idea for a movie was to have the band board a bus with a group of friends and set off across England, filming the high jinks that were bound to ensue. The Magical Mystery Tour, as the trip and the subsequent film were dubbed, was not as "magical" as McCartney hoped. With little planning, the tour ran into traffic jams, had no prearranged accommodations, and offered less-than-stellar filming opportunities. The resulting movie was then edited by each Beatle in turn, and the whole mess was sold to the BBC for release. The airing of *Magical Mystery Tour* drew 15 million viewers, but the reaction was decidedly negative. One *Daily Express* television critic declared it "blatant rubbish."

The next Beatles' film was the animated feature *Yellow Submarine*. Released in 1968, the movie was a contractual obligation to United Artists. Considered somewhat of a throwaway to Beatles' management, the animated John, Paul, George, and Ringo were not even voiced by the band members. But because of the striking animation and the inclusion of some new Beatles' tunes, *Yellow Submarine* was a critical and popular hit. The final Beatles' film was *Let It Be*, a semidocumentary of the band's struggle to make its last album. Shot in 1969 but released in 1970, *Let It Be* showed the band working together and creating music—despite the fact that the group had already fractured and was nearly defunct. The film sank— like the band—without much fanfare.

In the following article, Bob Neaverson discusses the impact of the Beatles' films upon their contemporary society and latter-day pop culture. Of significance to Neaverson are the ways in which the films changed the format of subsequent movie musicals, gave credibility to the British film industry in the 1960s, and influenced—if not gave birth to—the music video era. Neaverson is a lecturer in film and media studies at the University of East Anglia and City College, Norwich.

Television tour documentaries apart, the Beatles starred in or otherwise contributed to a total of five films: *A Hard Day's Night* (1964), *Help!* (1965), *Magical Mystery Tour* (TV movie, 1967), *Yellow Submarine* (1968) and *Let It Be* (1969, released 1970). Given that the group's first album was only released in 1963 and that they had effectively ceased to function as a unified creative force by 1970, that represents a considerable tally. Yet in the wake of their glorious recording career, the Beatles movies (and, for that matter, their promotional films) have been largely overlooked by the critical establishment. While some would maintain that this is not particularly surprising (the Beatles were, after all, primarily a recording outfit), their comparative neglect within film history has not been aided by the group's own reluctance to discuss the films, poor availability in the home video market, and the auteurist bias which still pervades much film history. The only two Beatles films which receive serious discussion are *A Hard Day's Night* and *Help!*, both directed by Richard Lester. I find this situation dismaying—not because I believe that the films reveal a group of great dramatic virtuosity (although Ringo isn't half bad in *A Hard Day's Night*) or that they should somehow be 'reclaimed' as 'classics'. (While I do believe that the films deserve reassessment, I'm not interested in entering into futile debates about what does or does not constitute a film's 'classic' status.) Rather, it is dismaying partly because the Beatles films constituted a vital part of the group's success in Britain and the USA and, perhaps more importantly, because they have exerted an enormous influence over subsequent pop musicals and videos. From a broader perspective, the films were also important to the sustained US investment in British cinema of the 1960s. For the most part, however, they seem almost to have been written out of history, revered by fans yet acknowledged only in passing by the majority of film historians and music journalists, and rarely investigated or discussed in any depth. . . .

BAND EXPOSURE AND PRODUCT LICENSING

In what ways were films important to the Beatles' career? From a purely pragmatic (economic) perspective, making films for international distribution was the easiest and most cost-effective way to ensure consistent global exposure and generate maximum box office and/or television exhibition revenue. Film production provided a more efficient means of public exposure than touring or making exclusive television appearances throughout the world, and was ultimately far less time-consuming for a group of the Beatles' global popularity. The commercial importance of making films became considerably accentuated in the wake of their unwillingness to tour after their final concert in San Francisco's Candlestick Park on 29 August 1966. . . .

As well as acting as an intrinsic source of box office revenue, the films also facilitated the sales of a number of other licensed tie-in products external to the cinema-going experience. . . . Indeed, while sales of recordings and sheet music were obviously highest on the agenda (United Artists agreed to finance *A Hard Day's Night* largely in order to obtain soundtrack rights), there were a considerable number of other licensed film-related products marketed—particularly in the case of *Yellow Submarine*, which boasted jigsaws, Halloween costumes, alarm clocks, mobiles, and, of course, Corgi's recently revived die-cast replicas. Although the Beatles movies can hardly lay claim to originating this exploitative approach, they were, like the ever-popular [James] Bond films, certainly important forerunners.

How did the films 'work' upon their audience? From a purely ideological perspective, the movies were obviously— and successfully—used to develop and confirm the Beatles' worldwide popularity. Perhaps more than any other broadcast media, their films were vital in communicating and showcasing the group's ever changing array of images, attitudes, ideas and musical styles. As well as re-affirming their recently aquired international status as recording artists, *A Hard Day's Night* helped to disseminate their then current visual 'look' to a global audience, and to develop their identities as four individuals (rather than a 'four-headed monster') who were by turns amusing, witty, sarcastic, profound and compassionate. In short, it imbued them with the individual personae so vital to the star-audience relationship, which were developed, in a variety of different guises, in their subsequent cinematic outings. While their early identities were to some extent consolidated in the fiction fantasy of *Help!*, their next film, the self-directed (and much criticized) *Magical Mystery Tour* crystallized their newly constructed roles as psychedelic figureheads of the emerging counter-culture. This was again consolidated, albeit in a somewhat more accessible and sentimental manner, by the benevolent and peace-loving cartoon caricatures of *Yellow Submarine*, while *Let It Be* documented a group of taciturn philosophers who, having turned the full musical circle, were now in an advanced state of personal and, to some extent, professional decay. Although the group had achieved a remarkable amount of international success prior to its forays into film, my suspicion is that the phenomenon of Beatlemania could not and would not have been either as substantial or as durable without the identificatory process afforded by cinema.

However, as well as serving an important role within the Beatles' own career, the films have also generated a broader influence. Economically and stylistically, the success of *A*

Hard Day's Night and *Help!* yielded considerable impact inside the British and US film and television industries. The international success of *A Hard Day's Night* contributed greatly to the influx of US capital into British film production throughout the 1960s, and the collective impact in that country of other successful US investments such as the Bond films and *Tom Jones* (1963) 'changed attitudes towards Britain, fostering a belief that London, rather than Paris or Rome or Hollywood, was the place in the world to make a film' [according to film historian Robert Murphy]. In fact, by 1967, around 90 per cent of British productions had some US backing. Consequently, this investment made a major impact upon the ever increasing production and distribution of British pop musicals and, in turn, upon the increasing profitability of the British recording industry in other territories, particularly the USA. . . .

Although the British Invasion was beginning to take place (through the Beatles) before either they or any other British act had produced a successfully exportable film, it is certainly true that the group's first two films, together with such imitative productions as John Boorman's *Catch Us If You Can* (1965), which starred the Dave Clark Five, played a significant, yet frequently overlooked, role in the dissemination of British pop throughout the USA. . . .

As well as compounding the success of the British Invasion and heralding a clutch of copycat movies, the first two Beatles films also exerted an important and lasting influence upon British and US television. The most emphatic demonstration of this was *The Monkees* television show which, from its inception in 1966, shamelessly exploited the style of the Lester movies, and featured a four-piece 'bubblegum' pop group whose coldly manufactured 'zaniness' was blatantly modelled on the Beatles' early presentation.

MUSICAL FILM AND POP VIDEO

While the Monkees came and (quickly) went, the most lasting legacy of Richard Lester's Beatles movies has been their formal influence upon the visual language and aesthetic values of the pop video. Prior to *A Hard Day's Night*, the majority of British and US pop musicals had relied upon the long-established tradition of song performance derived from the classical Hollywood musical. In the contemporaneous vehicles of Elvis Presley and Cliff Richard, the genre's central musical sequences were inevitably based around the presentation of lip-synched 'performances' of songs by a solo singer which, often combined with minimal onscreen backing sources (in the case of the Presley cycle, his guitar), essentially attempted to articulate the illusion of 'real', diegetic performance. Although such performances were usually, and often necessarily, accompanied by non-diegetic backing (the 'unseen' accompaniment), the underlying importance of this aesthetic was to reproduce the illusory spectacle of performance, as if to reassure the audience of the artist's 'authenticity'. *A Hard Day's Night* changed all that, and was arguably the first film of its genre to fully realize the *illustrative* potential of pop music. While the movie does include a good quota of more conventional 'performances', the 'Can't Buy Me Love' sequence midway through the narrative (which marries the song with footage of the group cavorting in a playing field) broke entirely with conventional approaches and, in the process, freed the musical number from its traditional generic slavery. . . .

This realization formed an important aesthetic precedent for subsequent pop musicals (including those of the Beatles), and, perhaps most significantly, pop video, which the group itself helped to pioneer from 1965 with the semi-diegetic promos shot by Joe McGrath for 'I Feel Fine', 'Day Tripper', 'We Can Work It Out', 'Ticket To Ride' and 'Help!'. The McGrath promos are important for two reasons. Financed by the Beatles' management agency, NEMS, they were the first independently produced pop promos made specifically for international distribution, thus pre-empting the arrival of the contemporary pop video age. Additionally, their style also anticipated that of contemporary video in their rejection, and partial mockery, of the conventional performance aesthetic favoured by TV shows such as *Top Of The Pops* and *Top Beat.* . . . Without the initial break with performance heralded by *A Hard Day's Night* and *Help!* the history of pop video could well have developed along very different avenues; and it is plausible to suggest that had the illustrative potential of the medium never been realized, the existence of the pop promo might easily have been condemned to an obscure footnote in histories of 1960s television. In this sense the Lester movies established an aesthetic precedent which was to become central to a medium external to that from which they evolved.

NONLINEAR NARRATIVE

Although critically stated in its day, *Magical Mystery Tour* has also been inspirational in its own ways. As well as its importance to the development of pop video, the film's radical rejection of conventional narrative logic helped to establish a precedent for later pop movies such as the Monkees' *Head* (1968). Frank Zappa's self-directed *200 Motels* (1971), the Who's *Tommy* (1975) and Led Zeppelin's *The Song Remains The Same* (1976). . . .

Perhaps, then, the film's single greatest achievement is that it played a key role in de-institutionalizing a genre which, to all intents and purposes, had been enslaved by the essentially conventional narrative form and predominantly conformist morality of previous pop musicals.

However, apart from its pivotal role in radicalizing the aesthetics of its genre, one might also argue that here too the formal and generic properties of *Magical Mystery Tour* influenced, or at least pre-dated, other genres of film and television. [Beatle critic Ian] MacDonald, who . . . is one of the few critics to recognize (albeit in passing) the film's importance, sees it as a prototype of the road movie genre which was inaugurated with the release of Dennis Hopper's *Easy Rider* (1969) at the end of the decade. Its links with British television of the late 1960s and early 1970s can also be seen; for example, elements of the film anticipated the style of comedy series such as *Marty* (1968–69) and *Monty Python's Flying Circus* (1969–74). If instances of *Magical Mystery Tour*'s surreal humour were inspired by programmes such as *At Last The 1948 Show* (written in part by pre-Python fledglings John Cleese and Graham Chapman), it might also be fair to acknowledge the formal influence of the Beatles' film upon the Pythons. This is particularly evident in the second series of *Monty Python's Flying Circus* (1970), in which the constant use of the non-diegetic insert of the applauding crowd seems directly lifted from *Magical Mystery Tour*. [Furthermore, Python member] Terry Gilliam's inventive surreal animation is very reminiscent of that used in both *Magical Mystery Tour* and *Yellow Submarine*. . . .

INNOVATIVE AND ADVENTUROUS

Similarly, the influences exerted by *Yellow Submarine* are no less important. As well as colouring the eclectic iconography of Gilliam's animation and proving a remarkably successful forerunner to today's product-orientated blockbusters, its chief contribution to British film culture lay in fostering a new subculture that Mark Langer has called 'animatophilia'. In tracing the film's influences, [Leslie Felperin] Sharman has argued that it was instrumental in popularizing animation within art-house exhibition inasmuch as its success encouraged programmers to buy in independent animated shorts which would otherwise have remained largely unseen outside the festival circuits. In addition, the interest garnered by the film instigated a boom in animation production which resulted in *Yellow Submarine*'s production studio, TVC, becoming 'one of the first large-scale training grounds for young filmmakers, including Diane Jackson, who was later to make *The Snowman*'

It is thus rather ironic that the Beatles' most 'decorated' film, the Oscar-winning *Let It Be*, should, in some ways, be the most formally derivative. If the animated pop musical feature that was *Yellow Submarine* can be described as one of the most original and adventurous British films of the 1960s, then the lineage of the Beatles' final film is much easier to discern, its minimalist verite approach clearly evoking the American direct cinema of Richard Leacock, the Maysles and D.A. Pennebaker, whose masterpiece, the evergreen *Don't Look Back* (1967), has had a huge influence over the pop documentary. What *Let It Be* lacks in originality however, it more than makes up for in voyeuristic magnetism. Although it is alone in having thus far bypassed a British home video release, it is in some respects the most absorbing of the five Beatles films through its fly-on-the-wall approach which provides a fascinating, if harrowing (and flawed), insight into the group's personal and musical relationships as Lennon, McCartney, Harrison and Starr struggle desperately to find a new direction. This interest was certainly not lost on contemporary fans, who flocked to cinemas despite the general hostility of press reviews. Today the film's cultural status rests largely on its claim to 'historical significance' as the only extensive footage of the group in rehearsal/studio mode. . . .

CONTINUING POPULARITY

Yet in spite of their critical and (in the case of *Let It Be*) commercial neglect, the Beatles movies continue to generate both interest and profit. Like the Marx Brothers comedies to which they were initially compared, the films still engage and, for the most part, amuse in a manner which seems to have transcended their period. The current popularity of the first three films in the sell-through home-video market would seem to echo this belief, suggesting that they have found second- and third-generation audiences. For five films which were made with no intention of achieving any sense of permanence, they have dated far more gracefully than many of their contemporaries, and there is no small irony in this. In the spirit of 1960s pop aesthetics, Richard Lester asserted repeatedly throughout that decade that he neither wanted nor expected his films to last. Today, he is justifiably amused by the irony of the situation, and although modestly accepting that he finds it impossible to be objective about his own work, suggests that they may have captured something more 'endearingly representative of their period' than a number of other films from the same era. Why do the films retain their popularity with audiences? The reasons, although both complex and numerous, relate predominantly to their continuous influence upon, and existence within, contemporary pop culture.

As the recently released (and heavily Lester-influenced) Spice Girls film attests, the pop musical is not quite extinct. Its popularity has however withered to the point where the release of a film such as *Spiceworld* (1997) is a genuine anomaly. Yet the formal language of the Beatles' films (and their promos) lives on most profoundly in the non-stop global jukebox that is music television. The fact that there have been no textual developments of equal significance since the group's movies has helped them to retain their youthfulness to new audiences, and while video-makers have discovered and employed all manner of new effects and technologies, the fundamentally illustrative, concept-based aesthetic of non-performance established more than 30 years ago by Lester is still very much in place. In addition, the fashions and range of images popularised by the Beatles in their films and promos have become strongly integrated into the post-modern collage of styles which pervades contemporary pop culture. The psychedelic clothing sported by the group in *Magical Mystery Tour* (and their cartoon counterparts in *Yellow Submarine*) has returned to the centre stage of indie pop fashion, and the mid-1960s look of *Help!* (corduroy and suede jackets, sunglasses and leather boots) has also become integral to the look of many contemporary bands. Indeed, to scrutinize the visual style of popular Beatles admirers like Oasis is to witness a near perfect synthesis of fashions culled from different periods of the Beatles' career and reassembled into a bricolage of styles which evokes a disturbingly schizophrenic sense of undifferentiated time. Likewise, the influence of the Beatles' recorded output has never been so prominent, and the Britpop revolution of the mid-1990s (of which Oasis are clearly key players) has at its core a nostalgic pastiche of the Beatles' abstract typical allusions and harmonic structures.

SOUNDTRACKS

But quite independent of the phenomenon of Britpop, the films' soundtracks have retained an eternal youth which has clearly been central to their longevity. While not wishing to enter into speculation about the complexity of reasons for the popularity of the Beatles as recording artists, a number of points are relevant when assessing the soundtrack albums. Like all of the Beatles' recordings, the soundtracks (with the possible exception of Phil Spector's 'revamped' *Let It Be*) benefited enormously from their production values. . . .

Beyond [the] clarity of sound lies the Beatles' music, and it is, ultimately, the compositions themselves which, perhaps more than any other factor, have been central to the movies' popularity; and consistent media exposure has ensured that they remain very much part of the 'now'. I would suggest that the central reason for their appeal is rooted in their durability. . . .

PARALLEL DECLINES

With the Beatles' official split in 1970 came the end of the world's most successful recording act. Significantly perhaps, it also paralleled the decline of large scale investment into British cinema. The degree to which the Beatles' split influenced this contraction is obviously unquantifiable, but while it has often been rather reductively explained as the result of the internal schisms, decreasing incentives and diminishing returns which characterised such late sixties productions as *Modesty Blaise* (1967), *Performance* (1968, released 1970) and *The Charge of the Light Brigade* (1968), only the most myopic of commentators would ignore the direct and indirect ways in which the two events were connected. On a purely cinematic level, the end of the Beatles meant that there was one less group of highly bankable British stars for the picking. Yet, even if the Beatles had never set foot in a movie studio, I suspect their demise would still have had some impact on foreign investment into British film.

After all, at the epicentre of the sustained US investment in British cinema were not only the home-grown talents of the film industry, but the country's distinction as a mecca of exportable pop culture, which encapsulated fashion, design, photography, the fine arts and, perhaps most importantly, pop music (most importantly, because pop was the most widely disseminated and 'inescapable' of these media, especially in the USA, where from 1964 onwards, it reverberated around the country as a stern and omnipotent warning to financiers that Britain's new found cultural status was not to be ignored). Throughout the decade, the Beatles were so much the nucleus of the cultural revolution that it is almost impossible to imagine it ever having happened without them.

Sgt. Pepper's Inside-Out

Allan F. Moore

When the Beatles stopped touring in 1966, each
member found time to pursue other interests. John
began an acting career, accepting a role in Richard
Lester's *How I Won the War*. Paul dabbled in painting. George flew to India and became immersed in a
lifelong passion for Indian music and religion. And
Ringo spent more time with his growing family. According to biographer Hunter Davies, the Beatles
were, each in his own way, trying to discover themselves—making up for the years lost to touring and
Beatlemania. It was at this point, in Davies's opinion,
that John, Paul, and George turned to LSD as a
means to further their self-knowledge.

LSD had been hyped in the counterculture as a
mind-expanding drug. Gurus such as Harvard professor Timothy Leary touted the drug as a gateway to
mental and spiritual awakening. But the Beatles also
became interested in Indian mysticism, which
George gratefully shared with his bandmates. Drugs
and spiritual enlightenment brought the band into
the center of the psychedelic scene that had begun in
America but was now making its way across the Atlantic. Soon the Beatles adopted a blend of Indian
and hippie clothing styles, and their trademark Beatle haircuts gave way to longer locks and mustaches.

In the midst of all this experimentation, the Beatles
recorded their most ambitious project to date. Released on June 1, 1967, *Sgt. Pepper's Lonely Hearts
Club Band* was a concept album designed around a
fictitious Edwardian circus show. Several of the songs
drew upon images from John's and Paul's youth.
Strawberry Fields and Penny Lane, for example, were
actual Liverpool locations near the pair's boyhood
homes—though the former, in song, took on the trap-
pings of an acid trip when fleshed out with John's

Allan F. Moore, *The Beatles: Sgt. Pepper's Lonely Hearts Club Band*. Cambridge, UK:
Cambridge University Press, 1997. Copyright © 1997 by Cambridge University Press.
Reproduced by permission.

lyrics. The entire album became an amalgam of
Paul's simple ballads, John's intangible mental wan-
derings, and George's spiritual musings. Infusing Indian music, symphonic brass, and rock and roll, *Sgt.
Pepper's* succeeded in combining the ideas of the individual Beatles and yet working as a seamless
whole. To many critics, this feat would never be accomplished again in the Beatles' recording career.

In the following selection from his treatise on the
album, Allan F. Moore discusses the inception of the
Beatles' masterpiece as well as the various songs
that comprise it. Dr. Moore is affiliated with the London College of Music and Media at Thames Valley
University.

There should have been nothing special about *Sgt. Pepper.*
April to June 1966 had seen the recording of the previous album *Revolver,* the Beatles' seventh successive UK No. 1,
whose diverse and innovatory material and approach to
production were to provide the impetus for journalists like
Melody Maker's Alan Walsh to bemoan the fact that pop music was growing up. In May 1967, prior to the release of *Sgt.
Pepper,* Walsh was complaining that the Beatles (together
with groups such as the Hollies and the Beach Boys) were
losing contact with their fans through their growing reluctance to tour, to appear on television and to be interviewed.
Indeed, the autumn of 1966 had seen what was to be the
Beatles' last tour, a decision that had been brewing for some
time (due in large part to their inability even to hear themselves on stage because of the incessant adulation) and
which was brought to a head by the nasty incident following
their apparent failure to accord 'proper' respect to Imelda
Marcos, wife of the Philippine dictator, on the Philippine leg
of that tour.[1]

FOCUSING ON ALBUMS

In late November 1966, they began recording work on
'Strawberry Fields Forever', which was intended to appear

---

1. By not attending a requested appearance at the Marcos residence, the Beatles unin-
tentionally slighted the dictator and his wife. When news of the "no show" reached the
public, angry mobs of Filipinos hounded the Beatles, attacking some members of the
band's entourage.

on the as-yet-unnamed eighth British album. In one sense, this was to mark a new departure. Having decided not to tour any more, the Beatles' entire musical effort could be devoted to the studio. While they clearly perceived this as a release, it necessarily created its own pressures in that their studio work would have to become valid in its own right, rather than function as an adjunct to other activities. This is not a simple issue, since the decision to stop touring was both caused by, and the cause of, the decision to become a 'studio band'. The context for this new departure was broad. The Beach Boys' *Pet Sounds* (Brian Wilson's response to the Beatles' earlier *Rubber Soul*) had received intense critical acclaim (the band were advertised as the 'World's no. 1 group' in *New Musical Express* of 29 April 1967), and Mc-Cartney particularly felt the need to go one better; William Mann's influential *Times* review describes the rather stagnant pool populated by the Monkees, protest music, the vaudeville revival, beat music and 'sticky, sweaty, vacuous' ballads; and years before the supposed incorporation of 'Baroque', 'Classical' and 'Indian' techniques within progressive rock [music critic] Bob Dawbarn was complaining of their intrusion in mid-1967.

In a second sense, it was business as usual, since this was merely another album. Brian Epstein and George Martin's 'master plan' of two albums (and four singles) a year had begun to slip, and a new album soon was necessary in order to keep the band in public view. At this stage, Lennon and Mc-Cartney were toying with the notion of taking as a theme (itself a novel idea) the exploration of childhood sites and memories in Liverpool. 'Strawberry Field' was, in fact, a children's home in whose woods Lennon used to play. December and January had seen the recording of two further songs on this theme: 'When I'm Sixty-Four' (actually written by Paul some years earlier, for his beloved father) and 'Penny Lane', a genuine locale whose street scene is partly of McCartney's invention. January 19 saw the first attempt at 'A day in the life'. McCartney's 'interlude' ('Woke up, fell out of bed . . . '), which was not inserted into the song until the following day, was built out of schoolday reminiscences, but Lennon's original verses simply retold three events: newspaper accounts of a survey of road holes in Blackburn and of the death of aristocrat Tara Browne, and Lennon's part the previous year in the film *How I Won the War*. The celebrated orchestral crescendi appear to have been McCartney's conception, apparently the result of being influenced by 'avantgarde' composers, particularly Stockhausen. Indeed, in his early review, Wilfrid Mellers found echoes of Stockhausen's *Momente* in the album's incorporated audience 'applause and laughter off'. At about this point, it appears that the theme of exploring childhood began to vanish. In any event, 'Strawberry Fields Forever' and 'Penny Lane' were released in February as a single, at the demand of Parlophone's US partner, Capitol.

EARLY TAKES

It was not until 1 February, and the first takes of 'Sgt. Pepper's Lonely Hearts Club Band', that McCartney realized the potential for creating a live show out of this fictitious persona, which could be inhabited by the Beatles themselves. The strange mixture of an Edwardian brass band transported to psychedelic San Francisco (and whose name was suggested to McCartney by those of various West Coast bands such as Jefferson Airplane and Quicksilver Messenger Service) itself rather typifies the age. George Martin notes that the military turn which this was given, particularly on the album cover, was partly a send-up of the US in Vietnam. We should not, however, read too much into a professed counter-cultural stance at this stage. The hippies' political 'programme' (if that is not too coherent a concept) was more deeply founded on the celebration of diversity, a celebration intrinsic to two primary cultural sources, the Hindu (model for British hippies in the wake of the Maharishi Mahesh Yogi) and the Amerind (model for US hippies). This diversity found ready expression in the non-contradictory sporting of both kaftans and military uniforms (by the Beatles among others).

The following week saw the first takes of 'Good morning good morning' and 'Fixing a hole', and any authentic historical location for Sgt. Pepper's band vanishes together with them. Lennon's 'Good morning good morning' seems to have taken its inspiration from his addiction to television (which was frequently on as background while he was writing), in particular a Kellogg's Corn Flake advert (the crowing cock) and the contemporary situation comedy 'Meet the Wife'. McCartney's 'Fixing a hole' developed out of do-it-yourself exploits at his newly acquired derelict farmhouse in

Campbeltown on the Kintyre peninsula in Scotland. At least, that is the official (i.e. McCartney's own) account. In tune with the times, however, the belief that the 'hole' to be 'fixed' was in McCartney's arm (i.e. with heroin) was widespread. Indeed, the album's only line which appears to have been intentionally provocative was 'I'd love to turn you on', from 'A day in the life'. Even here, though, McCartney claimed that they were trying to turn people on to the 'truth' rather than drugs, despite their own heavy usage of LSD and marijuana during this period.

OTHER INSPIRATIONS

February also saw the first takes of four more songs. Harrison's 'It's only a northern song' was jettisoned from the project within days, while 'Being for the benefit of Mr Kite', 'Lovely Rita' and 'Lucy in the Sky with Diamonds' were further distanced from any Sgt. Pepper persona. The lyrics for Lennon's 'Mr Kite' were taken almost wholesale from a Victorian circus poster bought by him a matter of days previously. Lennon's own views on the song's quality swung at different times from it being a 'throwaway' to its 'purity'. The description of the doughty Rita as a 'meter maid' was derived from an American friend of McCartney's, while the title of Lennon's 'Lucy in the Sky with Diamonds' was taken from a school painting by son Julian (aged four at the time). Much of the imagery in this derives from Lennon's love of the Goons (Peter Sellers, Spike Milligan, Harry Secombe) and Lewis Carroll: in interview McCartney suggested that for Lennon 'Lucy was God, the big figure, the White Rabbit', although [Beatle critic Ian] MacDonald argues that she was the '"lover/mother" of his most helpless fantasies'. . . . The acronymic reference to lysergic acid [LSD] was apparently, not initially intended by Lennon. . . . In each of these songs, we can see that the concern while writing is neither to know what the song is about, nor to recount a narrative or relate a message, but merely to work. A casual phrase or encounter will set off an idea which is then worked on, according to its own logic, but without the slightest care for any prospective audience. This is not to say that the Beatles were averse to preaching, of course, or to addressing intimate relationships, but it is a mistake to attempt to find a definitive message hidden within every set of lyrics. (This has caused problems for many commentators, though not necessarily for fans. . . .)

This refusal to preach is not the case with 'Within you without you', George Harrison's accepted contribution to the project, and the second of four songs which began recording during March. In 1965, Harrison had become interested in the congruence between LSD-induced loss of ego and that espoused by Hindu sects, and this was the first of many attempts to 'return from the mountain to the market-place'. Although both Lennon and McCartney showed passing interest in 1967–8, and though all later admitted disillusion with

---

CHANGING THE FACE OF POP MUSIC

In his autobiography, the Beatles' longtime producer George Martin discusses the band's revolutionary ninth album. According to Martin, Sgt. Pepper's Lonely Hearts Club Band *gave a new dimension to the Beatles' music and set higher standards for other record makers in the sixties and beyond.*

Sgt. Pepper's Lonely Hearts Club Band was a musical fragmentation grenade, exploding with a force that is still being felt. It grabbed the world of pop music by the scruff of the neck, shook it hard, and left it to wander off, dizzy but wagging its tail. As well as changing the way pop music was viewed, it changed the entire nature of the recording game— for keeps. Nothing even remotely like *Pepper* had been heard before. It came at a time when people were thirsty for something new, but still its newness caught them by surprise. It certainly caught me on the hop!

Pepper drove a splitting wedge through the heart of British pop; many see it as the watershed. By shutting themselves (and me) up in the studio for six months and doing their own thing, the Beatles put a question mark over what everyone else in the business was doing. The question was: are you making music, or just money? Do you blow musical bubble-gum, or play rock with a hard centre? Up until this point, the Beatles had been pretty much bubble-gum artists. With *Pepper*, they drew a line and crossed it.

The Beatles themselves never pretended they were creating art with *Sgt. Pepper*, or scrabbling after some kind of musical 'integrity'. They just wanted to do something different, and *Pepper* was it. Nowadays, when rock music in its turn has been commercially disembowelled, the distinction between the two forms of music is blurred. But it is still there, and *Pepper* caused it.

George Martin, with William Pearson, *With a Little Help from My Friends: The Making of Sgt. Pepper*. New York: Little, Brown, 1994.

the person of the Maharishi, Harrison's conversion had real substance, as reflected in his view of the audience. Responding to a journalist's question, 'having achieved worldwide fame by singing pleasant, hummable numbers don't they feel they may be too far ahead of the record-buyers?'; George thinks not: 'People are very, very aware of what's going on around them nowadays. They think for themselves and I don't think we can ever be accused of underestimating the intelligence of our fans.' 'Getting better' was another song sparked off by an odd phrase, in this case the title. In a conversation between McCartney and biographer Hunter Davies, McCartney acknowledged that it had been the only comment they could ever get out of Jimmy Nicol, stand-in drummer for a week of touring in 1964. 'She's leaving home' was taken from a newspaper article, although a few of the details, and the protagonists' motivations, were supplied by McCartney.

So, by mid-March, songs were being written in great haste in order to fulfil the requirements of the album. According to Davies, this was usual procedure for the Beatles. The early songs written for an album might well have developed from a lot of inspiration and rewriting, but towards the end it became 'simply' a hack job. Indeed, Davies's illustration, 'Being for the benefit of Mr Kite', was certainly not one of the last to be written, so we may assume that the practice of writing 'on the hop' accounts for a large proportion of the album.

LENNON AND MCCARTNEY AT WORK

While the reprise of 'Sgt. Pepper's Lonely Hearts Club Band' (a suggestion of [road manager] Neil Aspinall) would be recorded on 1 April, the last full song to emerge from the recording studio was 'With a little help from my friends'. It was written specifically for Ringo to sing (it was usual for him to have one track per album). With the characteristically Liverpudlian persona of 'Billy Shears', the song created the opportunity to reinforce the 'live show' illusion of the album. This illusion seems to have been intended without any irony, and certainly seems to have deceived a few early critics. Hunter Davies's 1968 biography gives an interesting description of the genesis of this song. His piece sounds like an eye-witness account but, although an active observer throughout the period, he is careful not to claim it as such. In any event, he describes a process wherein Lennon and McCartney worked together on the song, without a clear idea of where it was to go, or what it would be about—they began with nothing but the opening line, and simply repeated musical phrases over and over at the guitar or piano, throwing possible lines, and even single words, back and forth. Clearly, what was always of primary importance was the way it sounded, with precise meaning rather secondary. This process continued even in the company of a disinterested audience: friend Terry Doran (the 'man from the motor trade' of 'She's leaving home') and Lennon's wife, Cynthia. Composing was frequently interrupted by excursions into different songs (both their own and those of others), jokes and snack breaks. 'With a little help from my friends' seems to have fallen into place on their return from one of the latter, as if their combined subconscious faculties had been working on it in the mean time. The final verse of the song was written in the studio in this way immediately prior to recording the first takes (a not unusual procedure for the band since the label's ownership of the studio greatly lowered costs through avoiding rehearsal and recording studio fees). This, in large part, was the special strength of the Lennon-McCartney songwriting partnership. Although a particular song may have been principally the work of one writer (unlike this example), the other frequently contributed the most telling word or phrase which could turn it around (e.g. Lennon's 'it can't get much worse' in 'Getting better'). It is no exaggeration to claim that, on the dissolution of the songwriting partnership, neither writer alone was able to reproduce the strength of interaction (as McCartney may presciently have observed in *Abbey Road*'s 'Carry that weight').

NOTHING SPECIAL

The speed of work, then, was impressive. So much so that before the end of April (the album was not released until 1 June) the Beatles were again in the studio recording the title song to the film *Magical Mystery Tour*, a concept which had only come to McCartney on a flight a fortnight earlier. They were not even involved in the stereo mixes for *Sgt. Pepper*. Stereo was still a new development, and although all their songs were mixed in mono with great attention, the band were happy to allow George Martin free rein with the stereo mix. This did not create as much leeway as it might sound: in mixing from only four tracks, there is often little choice as to where to place and balance particular sounds. Even the running order seems to have been left up to Martin with the Beatles giving final approval, although they had played around with possible orders. Martin's lengthy rationale for the running order makes it clear that 'Side One' generally carried greater weight than 'Side Two' (many listeners would only listen to side one of an album, switching to another album rather than listen to side two), while the placing last of 'A day in the life' was purely pragmatic: nothing could possibly follow its greatly extended piano fade.

As I suggested, then, there should have been nothing special about *Sgt. Pepper.* Accounts of its genesis and architecture paint it as something of a mixed bag. In was not the 'all-time killer album' planned in meticulous detail from beginning to end. As Martin points out, the Beatles sensed a strong challenge from the Beach Boys' album *Pet Sounds* (and also the single 'Good vibrations' of 1966), both in terms of production values and songwriting, but such concerns were not evident in the manner in which *Sgt. Pepper* was put together. Contemporary media reports imply the Beatles were trying to keep their heads above the waves not only of the Beach Boys, but also of the Monkees, Jimi Hendrix, Dave Dee, Spencer Davis, Procol Harum, to name but the most prominent. The Beatles had been virtually incommunicado for months; more significantly, *Sgt. Pepper* was an album put together almost out of control, and, as such, it encapsulated the group's career, despite the efforts of Epstein, Martin, even McCartney. George Martin was to write nearly three decades later: 'By 1966 the Beatles were in a car that was going downhill very fast. This is not to say that their career was going downhill; but they were a media juggernaut that was increasingly out of their manager Brian Epstein's control—and everybody else's, for that matter. It wasn't so much that somebody was pressing the accelerator too hard; it was that nobody had their foot on the brake.'

The Rishikesh Excursion

Philip Norman

The Beatles thought of their decision not to tour anymore as closing a chapter in their history as a band. Manager Brian Epstein saw it as depriving him of a vital part of his job, and he became depressed. To remedy his mental state, he started seeking solace in drugs. He also began devoting his time to handling other acts in his NEMS Enterprises. The other entertainers in the NEMS stable, however, were not quick to garner as much attention as the Beatles had. Still, Epstein continued to work hard, and, to some observers, he seemed upbeat about the future. Concerned friends believed Epstein was working too hard. Eventually the stress and drugs caught up with Epstein. On August 27, 1967, he was found dead in his country house in London.

Only two days before the discovery, the Beatles headed to Bangor, Wales, to sit in the august presence of the Maharishi Mahesh Yogi. The Beatles first met the Maharishi only a few days previously during a lecture stop in London. The Indian guru then invited the band for a spiritual retreat in Bangor in which the four initiates could be indoctrinated into his philosophy of transcendental meditation. The Beatles accepted since George was already interested in Indian religion and John and Paul were looking for some kind of inner peace. The indoctrination was mutually beneficial since the Beatles were looking for answers and the Maharishi could derive credibility through the band's celebrity.

In the following excerpt from his history of the Beatles, biographer and novelist Philip Norman describes the band's early meetings with the Maharishi and their subsequent investigation and eventual

Philip Norman, *Shout!: The Beatles in Their Generation.* New York: MJF Books, 1981.

adoption of his mystical teachings. Though Ringo
was the least entranced with the spiritual guide and
his rhetoric, the Beatles as a whole were intrigued
enough to stage a trip to India in February 1968 to
again sit at the feet of the Maharishi. The Rishikesh
excursion, as Norman relates, was not as revelatory
as the band had hoped. Ringo departed after ten
days. Paul deserted on week nine, followed quickly
by John and George who just weren't finding the answers they wanted from the mystic. Back in England,
the band denounced the Maharishi as less-than-
divine and spoke of getting on with future projects.

In the week before August Bank Holiday, Patti Harrison read
that—unheralded, for once, by tube station walls—the Maharishi Mahesh Yogi had come to London, to deliver a single
lecture before retiring from his crusade and devoting himself to a "life of silence" in India. The valedictory lecture was
to take place at the mystic's hotel, the Park Lane Hilton, on
Thursday, August 24. Patti made George contact the other
Beatles and persuade them to attend.

The encounter, that Thursday evening next to Hyde Park,
did have an air of divine predestination. Amid the small audience of the faithful, four Beatles garbed as flower power
aristocrats listened while a little Asian gentleman, wearing
robes and a gray-tipped beard, described in his high-pitched
voice, interspersed with many mirthful cachinnations, an
existence both more inviting and more convenient than
mere hippydom. The "inner peace" which the Maharishi
promised, and which seemed so alluring to pleasure-
exhausted multimillionaires—not to mention the "sublime
consciousness" so attractive to inveterate novelty-seekers—
could be obtained even within their perilously small span of
concentration. To be spiritually regenerated, they were told,
they need meditate for only half an hour each day.

Maharishi Mahesh Yogi, despite a highly developed nose
for publicity, did not know the Beatles were in his congrega-
tion until after the lecture, when they sent up a request to
speak to him in private. There and then, acting as a group,
they offered themselves as his disciples. The holy man, for
whom "tickled" would be an insufficient adjective, invited
them to join him the next day on a course of indoctrination

for the spiritually regenerated at University College, Bangor, North Wales. The Beatles said they would go.

They did subsequently contact Brian and ask him to join the party. He, too, had been showing some interest in Indian religion. Brian said he had other plans for the Bank Holiday weekend, but that he'd try to get down to Bangor later during the ten-day course.

AT BANGOR

An incredulous orgy of press and TV cameras saw them off at Paddington next day, on the Maharishi's special slow stopping-train. As well as the Beatles, Patti and [Paul's girlfriend] Jane Asher, there was Mick Jagger—whose demon tones could currently be heard in a Beatle-inspired song unconvincingly titled "We Love You"—and Jagger's girl friend, Marianne Faithfull. Cynthia Lennon missed the train, held back by a policeman who thought she was a fan. "Run, Cindy, run," called John as she sprinted vainly along the platform.

It was the first journey they had ever made without Brian—without even the two protective road managers. John compared it to "going somewhere without your trousers." They all sat rather guiltily wedged into one first class compartment, afraid to venture so much as to the lavatory. They then had a second audience with the Maharishi, who occupied his own first class compartment, squatting on a sheet spread over British Rail's green upholstery. Once again, the holy being showed his marked propensity for mirth. He held up a flower—the first of many—and explained that its petals were an illusion, like the physical world. In a telling simile, he compared Spiritual Regeneration to a bank, from which its practitioner could always draw dividends of repose.

If any proof were needed of the sublime state of the Maharishi's mind, it occurred when the train reached Bangor, and a frantic crowd drew into sight on the little seaside platform. The Beatles suggested going on to a further station, then returning to Bangor by taxi. The Maharishi, to whom it had not occurred that the crowd comprised followers other than his own, told them to stay close to him.

That night, the Beatles, the satanic chief Rolling Stone and their female companions found themselves ensconced, with the Maharishi's three hundred other conference students, in the spartan bedrooms of a teacher training college. Later, accompanied by [friend and journalist] Hunter Davies, they went out to the only restaurant open late in Bangor—a Chinese. After a long and noisy meal, it was discovered that no one among the assembled millionaires had enough money to pay the bill. In London, they were never allowed to pay. Chinese waiters in a North Wales town clearly did not understand this. At last, with the waiters growing restive. George Harrison prised open his sandal-sole and produced a wad of £10 notes.

On Saturday, as the Maharishi addressed his followers seated on a couch, the Beatles formed an obedient line to his right. He agreed, with no apparent show of reluctance, to hold a press conference for the journalists who now swarmed over the college. The questions were hostile and satirical. The Beatles answered with such spirit that the Maharishi's regular disciples broke into spontaneous applause. It was here that the weekend's first major story broke. The Beatles used the press conference to announce that they had given up taking drugs. "It was an experience we went through," Paul McCartney said. "Now it's over. We don't need it any more. We think we're finding new ways of getting there."

One of the journalists was George Harrison, their old Liverpool *Echo* acquaintance—for Bangor is just in the *Echo*'s circulation area. Harrison was with them the next afternoon—Sunday—as, fully initiated into Spiritual Regeneration, they strolled around the college grounds.

"There was a phone ringing inside," Harrison says. "It rang and rang. Eventually, Paul said, 'Someone had better answer that.' He went in and picked up the phone. I could hear him speaking. 'Yeah,' he said. 'Yeah . . . ' Then I heard him shout, 'Oh, Christ—*no!*" [Paul had just received word of Brian Epstein's death]. . . .

ON TO RISHIKESH

In February [1968], in the midst of [the Beatles' business venture] Apple's gestation, John and George, with Cynthia and Patti, flew to India to begin their much-postponed religious studies under the Maharishi Mahesh Yogi. The advance party also included Patti's sister, Jennie, and the indispensable Magic Alex [Alexis Mardas, a gadget inventor who glommed on to the Beatles]. Paul and Jane followed soon afterwards, with Ringo, Maureen and a consignment of baked beans which Ringo had brought as insurance against the curry-eating weeks ahead.

The ashram, to which their pocket-sized guru mirthfully welcomed them, was not devoid of fleshy comforts. Situated in verdant foothills above the Ganges at Rishikesh, it accommodated the students of the Maharishi in stone bungalows, equipped with English hotel furniture, telephones and running water. A high perimeter fence and padlocked gate shielded its devotees from sightseers, beggars, *sadhus* [Hindu monks], wandering cows and the odor of everyday worship at the *ghats*, or holy bathing places, below along the river bank. The Maharishi himself occupied an elaborate residence equipped with a launching pad for the private helicopter in which the holy man would periodically view his well-appointed domain.

Apart from the Beatles, an impressive netful of personalities had been trawled to sit at the Maharishi's feet. They included Mike Love of the Beach Boys; Donovan, the English folk singer, and his manager, Gypsy Dave; and the film actress, Mia Farrow. All put off their pop hippy finery, the girls to dress in saris, the boys in *kurta* tunics, loose trousers and sandals. At Mike Love's example, both John and George started to grow beards. John even experimented with a turban, though he could not resist the temptation to pull "cripple faces" when wearing it.

The Maharishi took pains to ensure that ashram life would not be too stringent for his cossetted disciples. The chalets were comfortable . . . and the food, though vegetarian, was ample; there were frequent excursions and parties. The Lennons received Indian clothes and toys for their son, Julian, and George Harrison's twenty-fifth birthday was celebrated by a seven-pound cake. Obliging houseboys would even smuggle the odd bottle of forbidden wine into the Beatles' cantonment.

Even so, the schedule of fasting, chanting and mass prayer quickly proved too much for Ringo Starr. He left Rishikesh with Maureen after only ten days, complaining that his stomach couldn't take the highly spiced food and that he missed his children.

THREE BEATLES REMAIN

The others showed every sign of sticking out the course for its full three-month duration. Fleet Street journalists who had infiltrated the stockade reported seeing this or that Beatle seated contentedly at a prayer meeting, feeding the monkeys that inhabited the trellises or aimlessly strumming a guitar. It emerged that they were holding a contest among themselves to see who could keep up nonstop meditation the longest. Paul McCartney led the field with four hours, followed by John and George with three-and-a-half each. They were also using the unwonted peace and immobility to write songs for their next album.

At regular intervals, [road manager] Neil Aspinall would fly out from London to report the latest progress in setting up Apple, and the position of "Lady Madonna," the single they had left for release in their absence, Neil was also making arrangements for Apple Films to finance a production in which the Maharishi himself would star. "We had a meeting about it in his bungalow," Neil says. "Suddenly, this little guy in a robe who's meant to be a Holy man starts talking about his two and a half percent. 'Wait a minute,' I thought, 'He knows more about making deals than I do. He's really into scoring, the Maharishi.'"

Paul, who filmed most of his and Jane's nine-week stay, remembered Rishikesh as being like school—mock-serious, with giggles lurking always behind hands. "We thought we were submerging our personalities, but really we weren't being very truthful then. There's a long shot of you [John] walking beside the Maharishi, saying, 'Tell me, O Master,' and it just isn't you."

DEFECTIONS

It was in the ninth week, after Paul and Jane had decided to leave, that John himself began showing signs of restiveness, "John thought there was some sort of secret the Maharishi had to give you, and then you could just go home," Neil Aspinall says. "He started to think the Maharishi was holding out on him. 'Maybe if I go up with him in the helicopter,' John said, 'he may slip me the answer on me own.'"

By the eleventh week, despite trips above the Ganges in the Maharishi's helicopter, the answer still had not come. Furthermore, it began to be whispered—chiefly by Magic Alex—that the Maharishi was not so divine a being as he had seemed, and that his interest in Mia Farrow might originate in a region somewhat lower than her soul. Even George, the guru's most impassioned disciple, seemed to be having second thoughts. So, to Magic Alex's gratification and Cynthia's dismay, John decided they were going home.

He led the way into the Maharishi's quarters and announced his decision, characteristically mincing no words. The guru, for all his quick-wittedness, seems to have had no idea that the lights had changed. When he asked, "Why?" John would say only, "You're the cosmic one. You ought to know." At this, he said later, Maharishi Mahesh Yogi, the Great Soul, gave him a look like "I'll kill you, you bastard."

John, in fact, was convinced for a long time afterwards that the Maharishi would wreak some sort of Transcendental vengeance. He told Cyn it was already starting when, on the way back to Delhi, their taxi broke down, and they both stood panic-stricken, trying to thumb a lift as the Indian dusk and the myriad staring eyes closed in around them.

WE MADE A MISTAKE

The Maharishi, his teachings and flowers and Transcendental gurglings were dismissed as utterly as last month's groupie or yesterday's Mr. Fish shirt. "We made a mistake," Paul McCartney said. "We thought there was more to him than there was. He's human. We thought at first that he wasn't." Into another airport microphone, George concurred: "We've finished with him." The holy man was left in his mountain fastness to cogitate upon a mystery as profound as any offered by Heaven or Earth. Had the Beatles, or had the Maharishi Mahesh Yogi, been taken for the bigger ride?

CHAPTER 4

DISUNION

PEOPLE
WHO MADE
HISTORY

THE BEATLES

Apple Corps

Bruce Spizer

On a May 14, 1968, taping of the *Tonight Show*, Paul McCartney and John Lennon, who were guests that evening, announced the inauguration of their new business interest, Apple. The purpose of the new company, as outlined on the *Tonight Show* appearance, was to give aspiring artists, musicians, and filmmakers a chance to fulfill their dreams without —as Lennon put it—having "to go on their knees in an office . . . begging for a break." But the Beatles obviously had broader horizons in mind for Apple. Within a short time, the corporation's interests would include forays into music publishing, electronics, and fashion.

In the following article, Bruce Spizer relates the rise and near collapse of the Beatles business venture. According to Spizer, Apple Corps, as the parent company would be known, was partly devised to shelter the band's money from punitive British taxes. None of the Beatles, however, knew how to run a business once it was handed to them. Bad management and excessive spending forced some of Apple's projects to close quickly and nearly bled the corporation dry as a whole.

The creation of Apple also hinted at the coming decline of the band. Although John and Paul embraced the more experimental parts of the organization, Ringo and George were mainly interested in adhering to Apple's initial mission of finding and developing new talent. The band's time together was ultimately sacrificed to diverging interests. Apple, however, did survive the demise of the Beatles, though it could not hold to its original concept. By 1973, Apple had wound up its media projects and severed its contracts with other musicians. It focused exclusively on promoting the Beatles collective and

Bruce Spizer, *The Beatles on Apple Records*. New Orleans: 498 Productions, 2003. Copyright © 2003 by 498 Productions, LLC. Reproduced by permission.

individual music catalog. It remained in that state until the 1990s, when it began reissuing some of its back catalog of recordings by former Apple artists.

On June 20, 1963, The Beatles Limited was incorporated in the United Kingdom and assigned Company No. 764797. The corporation's shareholders were John Winston Lennon, George Harrison, James Paul McCartney and Richard Starkey, each owning 25 of the company's 100 ordinary £1 shares. In a move to reduce the huge tax burden facing the individual members of the group, a partnership named Beatles and Co. was established on April 19, 1967. Under the Deed of Partnership, each Beatle owned a 5% interest in the company, with the remaining 80% owned by The Beatles Limited. The partnership agreement provided that all of the income earned by the Beatles, with the exception of songwriting royalties, would be paid into The Beatles Limited. This substantially reduced taxes as the British corporate tax rates were significantly lower than the individual tax rates. Furthermore, income flowing into the corporation could be offset by corporate expenses. At the time this arrangement was set up, the Beatles had no idea how big those expenses would become.

By resolution dated November 17, 1967, the members of The Beatles Limited (John, George, Paul and Ringo) voted to change the corporation's name to Apple Music Limited. The name change took effect on December 4, 1967, with the filing of the appropriate corporate documents. A special resolution adopted by the members on January 12, 1968, changed the name again, this time to Apple Corps Limited, the company's current name. This change took effect on February 9, 1968.

Paul is given credit for naming the company Apple. In an Apple press release, managing director Nell Aspinall stated: "Paul came up with the idea of calling it Apple, which he got from René Magritte . . . [who] painted a lot of green apples. I know Paul bought some of his paintings in 1966 or early 1967.". . . Alistair Taylor, who at the time was with Brian Epstein's NEMS Enterprises, recalls McCartney telling him in 1967 that the Beatles company was going to be called Apple. According to Taylor, Paul explained that "A is for Apple" is one of the first things a child learns. Apple Music quickly developed into Apple Corps, which is a pun blending apple core and Apple Corporation. When [Capitol Records executive] Ken Mansfield asked Paul why the company was named Apple, McCartney replied "Have you ever heard anyone say anything bad about an apple?" . . .

RELATIONSHIP WITH NEMS

As early as Spring 1967, the group began meeting regularly with their advisors to discuss ways of spending their money to defer immediate recognition of income. Initial plans for the business followed traditional investment ideas associated with tax shelters, such as real estate, including a four-story building at 94 Baker Street that would later serve as Apple's first office. Other ideas, such as establishing a chain of card shops, were shot down by the group because they didn't want their name associated with "bloody greeting cards." Consideration was given to setting up a chain of record stores, but this idea was abandoned.

After rejecting a series of investment suggestions made by their accountants and other advisors, the group decided to enter into an area promoted by Paul—music publishing. Due to the numerous recordings and performances of Lennon-McCartney songs, Paul was well aware of how much money music publishers could make with hit tunes. Years later, Paul would increase his own massive fortune by obtaining the publishing rights to several songs, including the Buddy Holly catalog. But in 1967, the idea was for the Beatles company to develop new songwriting talent.

Although Beatles manager Brian Epstein had little involvement with Apple, his death on August 27, 1967, changed everything. John was the one who best understood the serious effect that Brian's death would have on the group. Shortly thereafter, Lennon confided in Alistair Taylor, "We've fookin' had it now."

The first changes came within Brian's management company, NEMS Enterprises. Brian's younger brother, Clive Epstein, was quickly appointed head of the company. Robert Stigwood, who had brought in new bands such as Cream and the Bee-Gees, left NEMS and took his acts with him, forming his own company, Robert Stigwood Organization. Stigwood's departure was prompted by the Beatles informing him that they would not accept him as their manager.

Unlike Brian and Stigwood, Clive had little interest in developing new talent, an idea embraced by the Beatles. In response to rumors that the Beatles would be leaving NEMS, the company's press officer, Tony Barrow, issued a statement in October that "NEMS continues to handle the management, agency and other business interests of the Beatles." The relationship would not last much longer. . . .

FIRST PROJECT

The first Apple project was *Magical Mystery Tour*, a psychedelic fantasy film featuring the Beatles. The movie was shot in segments without benefit of a script during September, October and November of 1967. Although Apple Films head Denis O'Dell wanted the movie to debut on American television (and was in negotiations with NBC and ABC), Paul insisted that the BBC be given first bite of the apple. The move backfired when the BBC showed the color film in black and white on the evening of December 26, 1967. The movie was savagely panned by the critics, causing NBC and ABC to drop their pursuit of the film. Rather than receiving a million dollars or so for U.S. broadcast rights, Apple had to settle for meager rental revenues from limited American screenings at college campuses. While the film was dubbed a failure at the time, it is now regarded as an interesting period piece depicting the free-wheeling spirit of the sixties.

Paul had pitched his idea for the movie in April 1967, to Brian Epstein, who would have coordinated the project had he been alive. With Brian gone, Paul took charge to ensure that his idea would become reality. Many of the logistical details were handled by Beatles road manager Neil Aspinall. His successful handling of this chore influenced the Beatles decision to hire Aspinall as Managing Director of Apple. This action was not made based upon his experience or qualifications. It was based on his loyalty and the total faith and trust that each of the Beatles had in Aspinall. The group hired Alistair Taylor away from NEMS to serve as Apple's General Manager.

PUBLISHING AND ELECTRONICS

Meanwhile, the Beatles were anxious to get their publishing company up and running. They hired another former NEMS employee, Terry Doran, to head Apple Music Publishing. Although Doran had no experience in the music publishing business, he had contacts and knew young and upcoming songwriters. Doran quickly signed George Alexander to a songwriting contract with Apple. . . .

Apple Music Publishing signed other songwriters, including Jackie Lomax, who would later record for Apple Records. His performance of George Harrison's *Sour Milk Sea* was one of the first singles released by the company.

The Beatles also ventured into electronics, placing their faith and money with a 27-year-old Greek television repairman, Alexis Mardas. John was particularly infatuated by Mardas and his inventions and dubbed him "Magic Alex." At first, they formed a company with him named Fiftyshapes Ltd. It was later renamed Apple Electronics and became part of Apple.

Magic Alex impressed the boys with his electronic toys. Some had potential, such as a device that enabled a person to listen to a record player through a portable transistor radio, while others had absolutely no practical value, such as a small metal box with 12 small lights that did nothing and was called a "nothing-box.". . .

The Beatles' faith in Magic Alex led to them requesting that he build a recording studio in the basement of Apple headquarters. Mardas boasted that his studio would have a 72-track recorder. This was at a time when 16 tracks was state-of-the-art and EMI was still limited to eight. The result was a total disaster.

FASHION

Apple Retail's first endeavor, a clothing store called "Apple," opened towards the end of 1967 on the ground floor of the group's Baker Street building. The store was initially run by Pete Shotton, who had no retail clothing experience, but had played with John in his pre-Beatles band, the Quarry Men. He was quickly replaced by a more-experienced John Lyndon in early 1968.

The bulk of the boutique's clothing was designed by a trio of Dutch fashion designers, Simon Posthuma, Marijke Koger and Josje Leeger. The three hooked up with British publicist Barry Finch and began calling themselves The Fool. . . .

While The Fool may have been good fashion designers, they were even better at spending Apple's money. They hired 30 art students to paint an elaborate mural over the outside walls of the Baker Street building.

The Fool's excessive spending was not limited to visuals.

Even though inside labels would remain unseen, The Fool insisted that their clothing be adorned with expensive hand-made silk tags. And, of course, Apple was expected to provide sufficient funds for The Fool to live a lifestyle appropriate for world class fashion designers.

The Apple boutique was launched with a splashy party on December 5, 1967, and opened for business two days later. Employees quickly noticed the lack of business controls and began raiding the cash registers on a regular basis. Customers came by to look at the beautiful clothes and the beautiful people, browse and shoplift. When neighboring businesses complained about the mural, Apple was forced to paint over it. The combination of The Fool's excessive spending, employee pilferage, shoplifting and sluggish sales led to losses approaching a half million dollars in six months. The Beatles decided to end the financial bleeding by closing the shop. At John's suggestion, the store opened its doors one last time on July 30, 1968, inviting the public to take what they wanted in a free-for-all orgy of legal shoplifting.

RECORDING

Having set up film, publishing, electronics and retail divisions, the Beatles finally turned their attention to what they did best —make records. Apple Records was set up with the same philosophy as the company's other divisions. It would discover and develop new talent. In addition, the Beatles hoped that many of their musician friends would switch labels and sign with Apple when their existing contracts expired.

Apple hired Ron Kass, an American who headed Liberty Records' British operations, to be president of Apple Records. Peter Asher, who had gained fame in the mid-sixties as half of Peter and Gordon, was brought in by Paul McCartney to serve as Apple's A&R (artists and repertoire) man. His job was to discover and develop recording artists for the label. His first significant signing was James Taylor.

Rather than hire an expensive ad agency, Paul decided that he could fashion a campaign to launch Apple Records. One evening he dropped by Alistair Taylor's home to kick around ideas. Paul came up with the concept of a one-man band who would be touted as an Apple success story. McCartney convinced Alistair that he would be perfect for the role.

Later that week, the pair went to a photography studio to shoot the ad. Alistair sat on a stool with a bass drum strapped on his back. He wore a harmonica around his neck and strummed a guitar. He was surrounded by a microphone, tape recorder, washboard tub, brass instruments and books. And, for the crowning touch, Paul purchased a bowler hat for Alistair. To add to the authenticity of the proceedings, McCartney insisted that Taylor sing. When Alistair protested that he was a lousy singer, Paul reminded him that he was being photographed, not recorded. As the photographer shot away, Alistair crooned *When Irish Eyes Are Smiling.*

The completed ad was placed in a number of music magazines and distributed as a handbill poster throughout London and the surrounding provinces. In America, the ad ran in the May 25, 1968, issue of *Rolling Stone.* Apple received over 400 tapes in two weeks. Hundreds more arrived in the following months. Although many tapes were ignored, Peter Asher did hire a staff to listen to them. According to Asher, "None of it was much good unfortunately. Out of the myriad of tapes we got in the mail, we didn't sign anyone.". . .

RELATIONSHIP WITH CAPITOL

Negotiations for the rights to manufacture and distribute Apple products in America began in February 1968, with Neil Aspinall flying to New York to meet with representatives of several U.S. record companies. The June 1, 1968, *Billboard* reported that five companies were vying for the rights. Capitol's relationship with the Beatles gave the company the edge.

On June 20, 1968, exactly five years after the formation of the corporation that became Apple, Capitol Records issued a series of press releases about the Beatles new venture. . . .

The August 17 *Billboard* reported that the Beatles Apple project was set to roll in America on August 25 with the release, through Capitol, of five discs. The initial releases would be George Harrison's *Wonderwall* soundtrack album and four singles, including a new Beatles disc featuring "two new songs written by them, *Revolution* and *Hey Judge.*" (The latter song was really titled *Hey Jude,* and the release of *Wonderwall* was pushed back to the end of the year.) The article reported that the Beatles were deeply involved in all of Apple's divisions, namely music, films, electronics and merchandising, and that a recording studio was being built in Apple's new London headquarters.

Propelled by huge sales of the Beatles *Hey Jude* single and *The White Album,* as well as Mary Hopkin's *Those Were the*

Days, Apple got off to a tremendous start. The February 1, 1969, *Billboard* reported that Capitol presented the Beatles with $2,500,000 in royalties for the last three months of 1968.

LOSING MONEY IN ENGLAND

While Apple's success in America was cause for celebration, things in London were a different matter. At an executive board meeting at Apple, Alistair Taylor gave the Beatles a heavy dose of reality. He informed the group that Apple was losing about £50,000 a week. The group's substantial revenue could not keep pace with the company's out-of-control spending. Salaries were too high, and employees were ordering expensive art and furniture for their offices and running up outrageous expense accounts. The Beatles were also guilty of excessive spending. And then there was the outright theft. People were stealing records, office equipment and even the copper stripping off the roof of Apple's Savile Row headquarters.

Alistair warned the group that if things continued as they were, the Beatles would lose their money within a year. He admitted that he and Neil Aspinall were not up to the task of running a complicated business such as Apple and told them that the company needed an experienced businessman such as Lord Beeching to take over and set things right. Beeching was the former head of British Railways.

Alistair got through to John, who, in a brutally frank interview with Ray Coleman in *Disc and Music Echo* magazine (January 1969), spilled the beans. Lennon stated that Apple needed streamlining and that if things carried on, "all of us will be broke in six months." He elaborated, "We can't let Apple go on like this. We started off with loads of ideas of what we wanted to do. . . . It didn't work out because we aren't practical and we weren't quick enough to realize we needed a businessman's brain to run the whole thing.". . .

Paul was also looking for answers. He was now seriously involved with Linda Eastman and discussed the problems at Apple with her father, Lee Eastman. Contrary to erroneous stories published over the years, Lee Eastman had no connection with the Eastman Kodak company. He had changed his last name from Epstein to Eastman in his early twenties. Lee Eastman was a successful attorney and expert in international copyright law. He owned some valuable music publishing copyrights and was an art collector. He brought his son, John, into his law practice, which was known as East-man and Eastman. When Paul asked Lee Eastman who he would recommend to fix Apple, Lee suggested his son John.

With Paul's blessings, John Eastman flew to London to survey the situation. He made some tax suggestions and advised the Beatles to buy NEMS, which was now owned primarily by Brian's estate. Eastman explained to the group that under their contract with EMI, 25% of their royalties were paid directly to NEMS. By purchasing the company, the Beatles would in effect receive their full royalties from EMI. Clive Epstein, who was handling Brian's estate and serving as chairman of NEMS, was interested in selling the company to obtain cash needed for payment of the substantial estate taxes due at the end of March. Eastman began negotiations with Clive, suggesting a purchase price of one million pounds. The transaction was to be financed by advance royalty payments from EMI.

ALLEN KLEIN MAKES HIS PLAY

Meanwhile, Allen Klein was getting ready to make his play to become the Beatles manager. Klein was an accountant who got his start in the music industry by auditing the books of record companies on behalf of musicians. Klein was aware that labels consistently underreported royalties owed to their acts. He became an expert at finding money already owed to artists. After successfully aiding Bobby Darin, Klein began picking up other clients. He became Sam Cooke's manager. This led to him securing the music publishing of Cooke's catalog for his management company, Abkco.

Although Klein had a questionable reputation, he got results. Not only was he getting his clients the royalties they were really owed, but also he was negotiating new recording contracts with higher royalty rates. Klein became the manager of British acts such as the Rolling Stones and Herman's Hermits. While he got the Stones a higher royalty rate than the Beatles, his acquisition of the American publishing of the band and other dealings left a sour taste with Mick Jagger and the other Stones. They parted ways, but not until Abkco had locked up the Stones sixties catalog.

Although Allen Klein had fantasized about managing the Beatles when the group first made its mark in America, he was a realist and knew nothing could happen as long as Brian Epstein was in charge. After Brian's death, he began his quest by meeting with Clive Epstein and Peter Brown. In his memoirs, *The Love You Make*, Brown found Klein "so foul-mouthed and abusive that I ended the meeting in a few moments and had him shown the door."

After hearing reports from London of John's claim that the Beatles were going broke, Klein renewed his efforts, this time going for the direct approach by securing a meeting with Lennon, which took place at the Dorchester Hotel in London on the night of January 27, 1969. Allen Klein made the most of his time with John and Yoko, impressing both with his knowledge of the music industry, the Beatles music and Yoko's art. John immediately hired Klein to handle his financial affairs and informed the other Beatles of his decision the next day. . . .

When Mick Jagger heard that Klein had met with John, he decided to brief the Beatles on the Rolling Stones' experiences with Klein, who was the band's manager. The Stones were in the process of terminating their relationship with Abkco, and Jagger apparently wanted to warn his friends about Klein. He agreed to drop by Apple to give a firsthand account of the Stones' dealings with Klein.

The details of Jagger's Apple appearance vary among those telling the story; however, all agree on one thing. Mick did not advise the Beatles to stay away from Allen Klein. Paul speculates that Jagger felt intimidated by the presence of the Beatles and was reluctant to give them advice. . . .

After completing the *Get Back* sessions, the Beatles met to decide who would manage their affairs. John convinced Ringo and George that Allen Klein was the man for the job. On February 3, 1969, the Beatles hired Klein to review their finances. Although Paul was against this decision, he chose not to fight the others, recognizing that the group needed to hire someone to straighten things out. McCartney was able to get Eastman and Eastman hired as counsel for the group. The February 15 *Billboard* reported that Klein had taken over the business affairs of the Beatles and Apple and that his function was to review and negotiate various business activities of the group. . . .

On March 21, 1969, Allen Klein was hired as business manager for Apple. He immediately cleaned house, firing nearly everyone in sight. Among the casualties were longtime Beatles confidant Alistair Taylor, Apple Records president Ron Kass and Magic Alex. Neil Aspinall was also on Klein's hit list, but the Beatles insisted that Aspinall keep his job with Apple. Derek Taylor was spared, apparently as a reward for helping set up Klein's initial meeting with John and Yoko.

Although Paul had reluctantly gone along with the decision to have Klein look into the group's financial affairs, he had yet to sign a management contract with Abkco.

On Friday evening, May 9, 1969, the group met at Olympic Studios for what was intended to be a recording session. The other Beatles told Paul he needed to sign the agreement because Klein was heading back to New York the next day. Paul told the others that the Beatles were the biggest act in the world and therefore Klein would take 15% rather than the 20% management fee called for in the contract presented to the group by Klein. He wanted to have his lawyer review the agreement on Monday. The others accused Paul of stalling and stormed out of the studio. . . .

The May 31, 1969, *Billboard* reported that Abkco, headed by Allen Klein, had signed a three-year contract to manage Apple and the Beatles. The article failed to mention that Paul refused to sign the agreement.

Ken Mansfield was disturbed by Allen Klein's firing of Apple Records head Ron Kass and informed Capitol and Apple that he was resigning. Kass was hired to run MGM Records and offered Mansfield a key executive position with the company. Although Klein had dismissed nearly everyone in Apple's London office, he flew to Los Angeles to discuss Apple's restructuring and attempt to reverse Ken's decision to leave Apple. . . .

Having failed to keep Mansfield aboard, Klein turned to his own company to fill the void. The running of Apple's day-to-day affairs was turned over to Abkco's Alan Steckler.

With his team in place, Allen Klein focused his attention to renegotiating the Beatles contract with the Gramophone Company Limited ("EMI"). Under the terms of the contract, which ran from January 26, 1967, through January 26, 1976, EMI had the exclusive right to manufacture, distribute, sell and exploit phonograph records and magnetic tapes of performances of the Beatles and the individual members of the group throughout the world. The Beatles were required to provide five singles and five albums. By the summer of 1969, the Beatles had all but completed their recording obligations under the agreement, thus giving the group leverage to renegotiate.

Klein informed EMI that the Beatles would not provide

any new records unless the group was given a substantial increase in royalties. After months of tough negotiations, a new agreement was reached. Under the 1967 contract, the Beatles were getting 39 cents per album. The new contract provided for 58 cents per album through 1972 and 72 cents per album for the remainder of the term.

As part of the agreement, EMI granted Apple Records, as licensee, EMI's rights to the Beatles for the United States, Canada and Mexico. This exclusive license covered all recordings made by the Beatles (either as a group or as individuals) during the term of the contract, as well as all records previously made by the Beatles owned by and available to EMI. Apple then entered into an agreement with Capitol under which Capitol manufactured and distributed the records and tapes for Apple. This brought significant revenue to Apple Records, who previously did not receive any income from the sales of Beatles records and tapes.

Abbey Road was the first album covered under the new agreement. Anxious to keep the money flowing, Klein had Apple (through Abkco) put together the *Hey Jude* album for the United States, Canada and Mexico.

Although Paul was pleased with the new recording contract negotiated by Klein, he never accepted Klein as his manager. By 1973, the other Beatles became dissatisfied with Klein, and their business relationship ended. They battled each other in court for many years. . . .

Throughout all the craziness, Neil Aspinall remained. As of . . . 2003 . . . he is still serving as Apple's Managing Director. Under his care, Apple made a triumphant return in the nineties, releasing six new albums, five of which sold in the millions.

"This thing called Apple" may not have worked out the way the Beatles intended, but Apple has ensured that the legacy of the Beatles music will be preserved for generations to come.

The Ballad of John and Yoko

Mark Hertsgaard

When avant-garde artist Yoko Ono joined John Lennon in the recording studio during the White Album sessions, many of the Apple studio staff felt she was an intruder. Of the other Beatles, Paul McCartney was perhaps the most put off by her presence since she usurped the close friendship between him and John. The Lennon-McCartney songwriting partnership also seemed threatened once John showed a preference for working through White Album songs with Ono's suggestions. Rumors began to circulate that Ono would be the agent of the Beatles' dissolution, though in hindsight, other factors had already begun to fracture the band.

In the following selection from his musical biography of the band, journalist and author Mark Hertsgaard asserts that the Beatles' ultimate demise was in part due to John and Yoko's romance. The coolness the band members as well as the Apple staff showed toward Ono upset John and helped distance him from the group. To Hertsgaard, John's love for Yoko was a type of worship that also contributed to his withdrawal from the Beatles. Hertsgaard is careful to acknowledge that even after Ono's appearance, the band still had great affection for each other, but the presence of a fifth Beatle proved another wedge that further divided the bandmates.

John Lennon once remarked that in the course of his career he had chosen to work with only two partners, Paul McCartney and Yoko Ono, adding proudly, "That ain't bad picking." To Lennon's great annoyance, however, he was virtually alone in this opinion, at least when it came to Yoko Ono. The

Mark Hertsgaard, *A Day in the Life: The Music and Artistry of the Beatles.* New York: Delta, 1995. Copyright © 1995 by Mark Hertsgaard. All rights reserved. Reproduced by permission of *Rolling Stone* Magazine.

world adored the artistic partnership of Lennon-McCartney, but it barely tolerated that of johnandyoko, as John christened them, and not simply because of resentment of Ono's supposed role in breaking up the Beatles. While John was "overawed by her talent" and what he called her "sixteen track voice," the public was more often bewildered and appalled by Ono's baffling kookiness and onstage shrieking. What in the world did he see in her?

One important exception was John's friend Pete Shotton. Although Shotton had ample experience with Ono's difficult personality, having felt the lash of her wrathful, manipulative arrogance more than once, he nevertheless maintained that "she was the best thing that ever happened to [John]." Not only was Yoko the love of John's life, maintained Shotton, she liberated him to be what "he'd always most wanted to be: an Artist, with a capital A." A second important exception, though only a partial one, was Paul McCartney. Affirming the latter half of Shotton's opinion, Paul said that Yoko had freed John to explore the avant-garde in ways that had not been possible during John's married years in suburbia. "In fact she wanted more," said Paul. "Do it more, do it double, be more daring, take all your clothes off! She always pushed him, which he liked, nobody had ever pushed him like that."

It was ironic that McCartney made this comment, for of course he himself had pushed John very hard during their years of collaboration, albeit in a very different way. Yet Paul was John's friend as well as his partner, and as a friend, he could not help but see how deeply in love with Yoko John was. . . .

FIRST MEETING

Paul's losing his partner was the last thing anyone would have expected when Yoko Ono first appeared on the scene. According to McCartney, it was actually he who met Ono first, when she asked him for old songwriting manuscripts for a project she was doing with avant-garde composer John Cage. Paul declined but suggested she check with his mate, John. Ono and Lennon met for the first time on November 9, 1966, in London, at the avant-garde Indica Gallery that McCartney had helped found, the night before an exhibit of Ono's work. Ono then pursued Lennon relentlessly, seeking patronage. Lennon's wife Cynthia recalled that Yoko not only barraged their house in Kenwood with dozens of phone calls and letters but would also wait in the driveway, no matter the weather, hoping to snatch a few words with John. Eventually she must have succeeded, for one day John instructed Shotton, who had been appointed a director of the Beatles' new company, Apple, to meet with Ono. When she nervously requested two thousand pounds to finance her next exhibit, Lennon told Shotton to grant it.

Shotton's recollections are invaluable to understanding the romance of John and Yoko, for he was at Lennon's house the night John and Yoko say they first became lovers, and he was the first person John confided in the morning after. Shotton had assumed that Yoko was merely a casual sexual conquest, a night of fun for John while Cynthia was away on holiday, but John's reverential demeanor the next morning quickly disabused Pete of such notions. "This is *it*, Pete," said John, gulping down a cup of tea and a boiled egg, in a hurry to return to Yoko upstairs. "This is what I've been waiting for all me life." He then asked Shotton to go find a new house where he and Yoko could live together.

John's Fleeting Enthusiasms

Shotton was flabbergasted. He didn't doubt his friend's resolve, but how long would it last? John had always been a man of intense but often fleeting enthusiasms. Moreover, he had been acting quite peculiarly recently, even by the eccentric standards of John Lennon. Barely twenty-four hours earlier, for example, he had decided in all seriousness that he was Jesus Christ, come back again. This revelation had come to John during an LSD trip, but he was no less convinced of it when he woke up the following day, and he was determined to tell the world. He insisted on immediately convening a meeting of the Apple inner circle—the three other Beatles, plus Shotton, Neil Aspinall, and Derek Taylor. When John announced his news, the others were stunned into silence; they could see that he meant it. Thus no one laughed or challenged his declaration. Rather, they agreed that this development was too important to deal with hastily; what was needed was time to absorb its significance and reflect upon its implications. And meanwhile, couldn't everybody use a quick drink or three?

John soon forgot his Christ fixation, as the others no doubt hoped he would. Yet the story is important beyond illustrating Lennon's colorful unpredictability, for it also sheds light on the other Beatles' states of mind at the time they learned of John's liaison with Yoko: To them, the Japanese artist must have seemed yet another example of John's fascination with the bizarre, a fad that would run its course, probably sooner rather than later, and be forgotten. They soon found out otherwise. The exact date of John and Yoko's first night together is unknown, but it was sometime in the latter half of May 1968, just days before the Beatles began recording the so-called White Album, officially titled *The Beatles*. Whether John introduced Yoko to any of the Beatles separately is unknown, but certainly everyone met her when they assembled at Abbey Road on May 30 for the first day of work, for John now insisted on having Yoko by his side at all times.

Yoko Becomes Involved

And not just by his side. Beginning with that very first session, Yoko also took part in the recording process. The song of the day was John's "Revolution," his most explicitly political composition yet. The Beatles eventually released three separate versions of "Revolution"—two appeared on the White Album and one as the B-side to the "Hey, Jude" single—but the two White Album versions actually began life as a single track. It was that track the Beatles were taping this day; its first four minutes were the slow guitar-shuffle later titled "Revolution 1," its last six minutes the chaotic instrumental and vocal jamming that became the montage titled "Revolution 9." Not until take eighteen was the freak-out part added, however; until then, each take had averaged only five minutes in length and concentrated solely on the song proper. But for some reason, take eighteen just kept going, the other Beatles bashing away on their various instruments as John and Yoko screamed and moaned and Yoko offered such enigmatic utterances as "You become naked.". . .

George, Paul, and Ringo added various overdubs to the ten-minute version of "Revolution" during the June 4 session as well, but two days later John and Yoko took the last six minutes of the take and began adding the many sound effects and tape loops that would transform it into the baffling "Revolution 9." Although George Harrison helped briefly, this recording was essentially John and Yoko's baby; Paul and Ringo did not participate, and Paul apparently disapproved of its being included on the White Album at all. This divergence of opinion was a good illustration of McCartney's remark about his and Lennon's differing attitudes about avant-garde work. Certainly Paul had no animus toward experimental recordings; as [Beatles' chronicler Mark] Lewisohn points out, Paul had led the Beatles' creation of a similar sound montage some seventeen months earlier, in January 1967. But that montage had been given to a London theater group, not released on record as part of the Beatles' formal body of work, as John proposed for "Revolution 9." But John, fortified now by Yoko's example and encouragement, would have it no other way.

Yoko Was There to Stay

As the Beatles moved on to subsequent White Album songs, beginning with Ringo's first solo composition, "Don't Pass Me By," it became increasingly clear that Yoko was there to stay. John's message to the rest of the Beatles recording team, George Martin recalled, was "Yoko is now part of me. In other words, as I have a right and left hand, so I have Yoko, and wherever I am, she is. That was a bit difficult to deal with. . . . To begin with, everyone was irritated by it." And not least because Ono did not merely keep John company in the studio, she also weighed in freely with comments and criticisms of the Beatles' work. By her own admission, she knew nothing about rock 'n' roll music, but that didn't stop her. When the Beatles were recording John's "Sexy Sadie," for example, Yoko interjected after one take that she thought they could do better. John, caught between his new love and his longtime mates, quickly stepped into the breach, saying, "Well, maybe *I* can."

John regarded Yoko as his artistic equal, if not superior, but it was plain that he was a minority of one in this respect, even if the other Beatles were careful not to say so directly. (The closest any of the Beatles inner circle came to speaking on the record about Yoko's musical abilities was George Martin, who commented after the Beatles broke up that Yoko Ono was not a substitute for Paul McCartney any more than Linda Eastman was a substitute for John Lennon.) John took the Beatles' coolness toward Yoko as a personal affront, conveniently overlooking that it was he who was changing the rules on *them.* Prior to Yoko, outsiders had generally been prohibited from eavesdropping on the Beatles in the studio; even close associates like Brian Epstein and publisher Dick James were encouraged to transact their business and leave. Now John was not only unilaterally ignoring these strictures, he was all but installing Ono as a de facto member of the group. Her constant presence and frequent intrusions annoyed the other Beatles, undermining the light-hearted togetherness and extraordinary synergy that had always been so vital to their studio magic. Lewisohn, not a writer given to speculative or pejorative judgments, has observed that the union of John and Yoko "had an undeniably negative bearing on the functioning of the Beatles as a unit,"

"WE'RE FRIENDLY FREAKS"

In an interview in London in 1969, John Lennon responded to questions about his relationship with Yoko Ono. Below is an excerpt from that interview in which Lennon acknowledges how he and Ono turned their private lives into public statements.

QUESTION: What you're saying is that as your private lives are going to be under scrutiny anyway, you might just as well play the game and turn it to your own devices, which in this case, is to push peace.

JOHN LENNON: That's it, Everybody's talking about it, but why aren't they really *saying* it? The queens and prime ministers and all the people in the public eye. Why don't they talk about it all the time? Instead of saying we *might* have a meeting, about a meeting, about a meeting to talk about it. It's like a dirty word. Especially in America. The radicals are saying, "Kill the pigs!" The establishment knows how to play the game violence, they've been playing it for millions of years. The radicals are never going to win.

QUESTION: Your relationship with Yoko in the early period, the nude photos on your *Two Virgins* LP and your honeymoon sleep-in, almost seems rather aggressive. As if to say, "I'm going to live the way I like and I want everybody to know it!"

JOHN: No, but see, if I had tried to have a honeymoon in secret, it would have been like Jackie Kennedy, you know. She tried the secret honeymoon, but it didn't work. They didn't get one, the press got it and it became a public honeymoon. So instead of fighting it, we joined up. All we did was use that event, which would have been in the press anyway, to get the word *peace* in whatever articles they wrote. And also to be on the front pages instead of other freaks. We're friendly freaks, that's all.

Geoffrey and Vrnda Giuliano, *Things We Said Today: Conversations with the Beatles*. Holbrook, MA: Adams Media, 1998.

for it "inhibited the others and made them feel uncomfortable and ill at ease in what had always been their ideal environment and refuge away from the madness outside."

JOHN'S INFATUATION

John being John, he apparently thought he had the right to do whatever he wanted; the Beatles, after all, were his group. And John being in love with Yoko, he could not fathom how anyone could fail to share his worshipful attitude toward her, both as a woman and as an artist. Rejecting John's assertions that the staff at Apple hated Yoko, Derek Taylor said, "No one in this building *hates* her. *Hate!* That's a very strong accusation and an extreme assumption. I can't say as I blame him for thinking that sometimes, but the reason he feels that way is because we don't *love* her." John's feelings for Yoko were so obsessive that he felt compelled to warn Paul—quite unnecessarily, Paul later emphasized—not to make a play for her. And Yoko herself later explained that the reason she accompanied John everywhere at Abbey Road, even into the toilet, was not because she wanted to, but because John was afraid to leave her alone in a roomful of men, since surely they would desire her as much as he did.

To John, Yoko was "this goddess of love and the fulfillment of my whole life." After years of feeling that no one was in his tree, he was ecstatic to discover someone who was "as barmy as me!" In John's eyes, he and Yoko were so much alike that she was "me in drag." Each had an eccentric, alienated, irrepressible perspective on reality that left them feeling alone in the world, "with a real need to do something to act out your madness," as Yoko put it. Thus they recognized each other as soulmates, sharing a connection so deep and transcendent that even John's wife had to acknowledge it. When she walked in on John and Yoko after their first night together, Cynthia recalled, "I knew immediately I saw them together that they were right for each other. I knew I'd lost him. . . . It was a meeting of two minds and nobody could fight that."

John claimed in one story that he and Yoko had been on the same wavelength from the very first time they met, some eighteen months before they apparently became lovers. When he offered her an imaginary five shillings to hammer an imaginary nail into one of her art pieces at the Indica Gallery, said John, "She got it and I got it and the rest, as they say in all the interviews we do, is history." But John told a lot of stories, and like most people he believed what he liked to believe, especially when it came to him and Yoko. Perhaps it did happen the way John said it did, for him anyway; but then he was the one that fell for her, not vice versa. In the very interviews that John referred to, for example, one does not find Yoko talking about falling in *love* with John, certainly not in the passionate, all-consuming sense that he did with her. For her, the attraction seemed to be more a matter of companionship and intellect; she had finally met someone who understood who she was, and loved her for it. He, on the other hand, had met "Don Juan," his spiritual guru.

MOTHER YOKO

Yoko was a mother figure to John, as she herself admitted, filling the gaping hole left in John's life after the double loss of his biological mother. "I was probably the successor to Aunt Mimi," Ono told Lennon biographer Ray Coleman. John had been the boss in previous relationships, often imposing his will through physical violence. The lines "I used to be cruel to my woman / I beat her and kept her apart / From the things that she loved" in *Sgt Pepper*'s "Getting Better" were autobiographical, John later confessed, adding, "I will have to be a lot older before I can face in public how I treated women as a youngster." Although John abused Cynthia more than once, Yoko denied that he ever hit her, and it is unlikely she would have stood for such behavior; she was the dominant one in this relationship.

It was a role she had been accustomed to since childhood. Born into a wealthy Tokyo family, she had grown up in a house with dozens of servants; at school, she forced her classmates to vote again when she wasn't given the role she wanted in the school play. As soon as she realized how smitten John was with her, recalled Pete Shotton, the nervousness Yoko had initially displayed evaporated and she revealed herself as "a strong-willed, domineering tigress.". . .

Although John denied the oft-made accusation that Yoko controlled him, the evidence is difficult to interpret any other way. Referring to the famous photo of John and Yoko that was taken the day before his death, showing a naked John curled in the fetal position around a distant Yoko, critic Robert Christgau commented, "As both of them were happy to make clear to Annie Leibovitz's camera, Yoko encouraged in her husband an infantile or even fetal dependence." Moreover, John was the first to admit that it was *Yoko* who kicked *him* out prior to their separation in 1973 (though he was silent about her dispatching their twenty-three-year-old Chinese secretary, May Pang, to serve as her eyes, ears, and sexual substitute during John's notorious "lost weekend" of drunken rowdiness). Furthermore, it was John who begged Yoko repeatedly to let him return. But she was the teacher who "taught me everything I fucking know," he said, and he was the pupil. She didn't let him come back, John said, until he had learned what he was supposed to learn.

JOHN'S REJUVENATION

In one of his last songs, "Woman," John professed that he would be forever in Yoko's debt. She had literally saved his life. Specifically, she had woken him up and liberated him from the suffocating self-indulgence and lethargy he associated with being a Beatle. "That's how the Beatles ended," John later maintained. "Not because Yoko split the Beatles, but because she showed me what it was to be Elvis Beatle and to be surrounded by sycophants and slaves who are only interested in keeping the situation as it was. And that's a kind of death." As usual, John was overstating the point, and in any case it was not the other Beatles' fault that the world surrounded them with madness. But listen to the love songs on John's *Imagine* album, where he sings that "for the first time in my life . . . I see the wind / Oh, I see the trees," and his rejuvenation is unmistakable. He is experiencing life anew, as if reborn.

Yoko also helped John return to the outrageous, impassioned, devil-may-care abandon of his youth. Although he and Yoko were sincere about their peace campaign, John confessed to Shotton that many of their public events—their nude album cover, their bed-ins, the news conferences they held from inside bags—were simply adult versions of the practical jokes John and Pete used to play as kids, except that John and Yoko now passed them off as avant-garde art. If the outside world blamed Yoko for leading John astray, those who knew him well recognized that in fact it was "just John being John," as Ringo put it.

If Yoko Ono did not directly cause the disbanding of the Beatles, she plainly was the catalyst that initiated John's inexorable withdrawal from the group. Reflecting on the Beatles' breakup, Paul later said, "Looking back, it was largely that John needed a new direction that he went into head-long, helter skelter. . . . He wanted to live life, do stuff and there was no holding back with John. And it was what we all admired him for. So we couldn't really say: 'Oh, we don't want you to do that, John. Stay with us.' You'd feel so wimpy. It *had* to happen." John agreed: "The old gang of mine was over the moment I met her. I didn't consciously know it at the time, but that's what was going on."

Nevertheless, despite the tensions that arose during the recording of the White Album, there remained a lot of affec-tion between John and the other Beatles. While rehearsing "Hey, Jude" in front of television cameras that July, for ex-ample, John teased Paul after one take by intoning in a mock-sentimental voice, "Well, I felt closer to it that time, Paul, I felt closer to it." When Ringo complained that he kept getting his trousers caught in his drum kit, John shot back, "Take 'em off!" And during a live televized performance of the song, an unmistakable look of loving friendship passed between John and Paul after John tried to make Paul break into laughter in the middle of his vocal. These are the kinds of moments that give credence to what John later hinted at separately: that he would not necessarily have chosen to break completely from his three longtime friends and part-ners. But on the other hand, if he did have to choose, there was no doubt which partnership was most important to him. "You see, I presumed that I would just be able to carry on and just bring Yoko into our life [as Beatles]," John ex-plained in 1970. "But it seemed that I had to either be mar-ried to them or Yoko, and I chose Yoko, and I was right."

Paul's Rumored Death and the Beatles' Real Demise

Nicholas Schaffner

In December 1968, Paul McCartney was eager to get the band back together as a unit. Although they had previously vowed to end concert touring, Paul hoped to persuade the Beatles to perform on television. The show would feature the band demonstrating new songs for an upcoming album. The Beatles did agree to give the project a shot, but by the time the re-hearsals came around, the group began squabbling. Paul's grand idea fell apart. The rehearsals, however, were filmed, and the "Get Back" sessions—named after the first released single—moved sluggishly ahead. Infighting, delays, and the constant presence of the cameras took their toll over the next few months, and the Beatles all but abandoned the proj-ect. Eventually the recording tapes would end up with producer Phil Spector in 1970. Spector, famous for his signature "wall of sound" production tech-niques, reworked the "Get Back" sessions with sym-phonic overdubs and gave back to the Beatles a new album called *Let It Be*. The overwrought record was not loved by the Beatles or the critics, but by then the band members were much more concerned with their forthcoming solo projects.

Let It Be was something of a Beatle epitaph. By 1969, John, Paul, George, and Ringo were estranged. They were not making public appearances together —nor alone for that matter. It was the absence from the public eye that fueled one of the more intriguing legends in Beatles history. In October of that year, rumors circulated that Paul McCartney was dead. According to clues laced through Beatles songs and record covers, Paul had not passed recently but had been killed in a car accident in 1966. To account for his appearances after the fact, the rumormongers argued he had been replaced by a twin. Although Paul, himself, assured his fans that he was alive and well, skeptics remained convinced of a cover-up.

In the following article, writer and performer Nicholas Schaffner discusses the rampant "Paul Is Dead" rumor as something of a harbinger of the band's ultimate demise. The same lack of a unified band presence that seemingly endorsed the rumor, Schaffner asserts, signaled the collapse of the collective musical entity. On April 9, 1970, Paul—or his supposed twin—announced to the press that he had resigned from the band. It was merely an official gesture that made public something which already had passed—the end of the Beatles.

On October 12, 1969, disk jockey Russ Gibb of WKNR-FM (Detroit's "underground" station) received an eerie phone call, which advised him to listen closely to the fade-outs of certain Beatles numbers, and to play others backward. Following instructions, Gibb and his listeners found (among other "clues") that John mutters "I buried Paul" at the end of "Strawberry Fields Forever," and that "Revolution 9"'s oft-intoned words "number nine, number nine" become "turn me on dead man, turn me on dead man" when one spins the White Album counterclockwise. By the same process, the message "Paul is dead man, miss him, miss him" emerges from the gibberish sandwiched between "I'm So Tired" and "Blackbird." Gibb, smelling a dead, er, Beatle, became the first of many vocal promulgators of Paul's untimely death.

MORE CLUES

Two days later *The Michigan Daily* ran a review of *Abbey Road* by Fred LaBour that took the form of an obituary, illustrated with a gruesome likeness of Paul's severed head. According to LaBour, the L.P. cover shows the Beatles leaving a cemetery dressed as a minister (John), an undertaker (Ringo), and a gravedigger (George). Paul is not only out of step with the others, but barefoot, as British corpses supposedly are prone to be buried. A cigaret in his right hand confirms that this is an imposter for the left-handed McCartney. The license plate of the parked Volkswagen spells out Paul's age: 28 IF he had lived.

One and one and one is three, concluded LaBour, who also cited corroborating "evidence" on earlier L.P. sleeves. *Sgt. Pepper* shows a grave, with yellow flowers shaped as Paul's four-stringed bass guitar. A hand is extended over McCartney's head—another omen of death. On page three of the *Magical Mystery Tour* picture book, Paul sits in front of a sign reading "I WAS"; two flags are displayed over his head, in the manner of military funerals. On page 23, Paul sports a black carnation; the other three Beatles' are red.

Soon afterward, Alex Bennett of WMCA-AM (a highly above-ground New York station) turned the controversy into the prime topic of his talk-show (after receiving a call from one Lewis Yager, who claimed to have been awakened in the night by the screams of a Beatlemaniacal girlfriend to whom McCartney's dire fate had been revealed in a dream). Not to be outdone, Bennett's counterpart on WABC quickly did the same. It was only a matter of days before the increasingly complicated tale of Paul's decapitation had swept across the North American airwaves to become the Number One topic of discussion and conjecture on campuses and in the "alternative" press.

QUICK DENIALS

A slew of sick novelty records (among them "St. Paul" by Terry Knight, the man who would soon bless the world with Grand Funk) were hurriedly recorded to cash in on the macabre fad. There was even a T.V. special, set in a courtroom presided over by famed defense lawyer F. Lee Bailey. The motley crew of "witnesses" included Allen Klein [CEO of Apple] and Peter Asher, claiming that Paul was alive and well—with Russ Gibb and his fellow ghouls, armed with the paraphernalia of the "evidence," to demonstrate the contrary. Mr. Bailey ruled that it was up to viewers to draw their own conclusions.

Meanwhile, Bennett flew to London to round up more witnesses. Paul's purported undertaker was ambivalent ("I'm not going to say anything because nobody believes me when I do," said Ringo) but photographer Ian Macmillan denied that there was any intentional symbolism on the *Abbey Road* jacket. Each Beatle was only wearing his usual 1969 finery, and as it was a warm day, McCartney had taken off his shoes. The 28 IF Volkswagen just happened to be parked there.

The Paul-Is-Dead buffs, however, found these explanations unsatisfactory. They ignored Jeanne Dixon, America's best-selling soothsayer, who divined that Paul was still with us. They didn't believe Lennon either, who said that the message at the end of "Strawberry Fields" was actually "cranberry sauce." When it was pointed out that McCartney was only 27 IF still alive, the ghouls countered by citing certain Asian countries where people are given a free extra year to account for time spent in the womb. And when—to all appearances—Paul himself finally emerged from Scottish seclusion ("Reports of my death are greatly exaggerated," he declared. "If I were dead I'd be the last to know."), his statements were scoffed at as the words of an imposter.

Each denial, in fact, was branded another link in the conspiracy; and the clues continued to proliferate. Sleuths all over America, delighted at the chance to put their Beatleology to practical use, peered at album covers through mirrors and magnifying glasses, and played the records themselves in every imaginable direction and speed.

Thanks to the demand for clean copies of the evidence, *Sgt. Pepper* and *Magical Mystery Tour*, off the charts since February, put in strong re-appearances. Exulted Capitol Records vice-president Rocco Catena: "This is going to be the biggest month in history in terms of Beatle sales." Small wonder both Capitol and Apple reacted to reports of Paul's death with respectful silence.

SUPPOSED ACCIDENT

As is generally the case with rumors, there were as many variations as there were tellers. But most agreed that the accident occurred in November 1966 (probably on the ninth, a "stupid bloody Tuesday"). Paul had stormed out of the Abbey Road recording studio, upset over a spat with the other Beatles. He took a spin in his Aston Martin (shown sitting in a doll's lap on the *Sgt. Pepper* jacket) and "blew his mind out in a car/he didn't notice that the lights had changed."

The accident, which "A Day in the Life" chronicles in detail, is also alluded to in "Magical Mystery Tour" (". . . dying to take you away . . .") and "Don't Pass Me By"; and "Revolution 9" features the sounds of an appalling car crash. McCartney's head was severed from its body, and the Beatle was Officially Pronounced Dead (the inside of the *Sgt. Pepper* sleeve shows him wearing an O.P.D. armpatch) on Wednesday morning at five o'clock (a phrase that George's superimposed likeness clearly points out on the *Sgt. Pepper* lyric sheet; in the same picture Paul's back is turned).

So then whose dulcet tones are heard on such songs as "She's Leaving Home" and "Magical Mystery Tour"? Well, or so the story goes, the other three Beatles conspired, for a giggle, to "cover up" this information from the general public. To give the impression of business as usual, the winner of a Paul McCartney look-alike contest was assigned plastic surgery and the task of filling a dead man's shoes. Fortunately for John, George, and Ringo, this William Campbell was also a McCartney sound-alike, with a knack for composing such poignant McCartneyesque ballads as "Hey Jude" and "Fool on the Hill."

Meanwhile—and this is the part of the story that people found easiest to swallow—the Beatles began planting a myriad of clues on each subsequent album, to test the fans' perceptiveness. John's "I Am the Walrus" was just one of many songs said to be pregnant with intrigue. Its subtitle—"No You're Not Said Little Nicola"—supposedly established that the Walrus was someone other than Lennon. The later "Glass Onion," of course, confirmed who that someone was: "The Walrus Was Paul." In the *Magical Mystery Tour* booklet, the walrus figure appears dressed in black. In Greek, it was claimed, "walrus" means "corpse." The record fades out to a reading of a death scene from Shakespeare's *King Lear.*

Truly, the Paul-Is-Dead saga boasted enough literary references and multilingual puns to do James Joyce proud. As a matter of fact, one erudite Beatlemaniac detected a clue in "I Am the Walrus"'s "goo goo goo joob" chorus; in *Finnegan's Wake* these are Humpty Dumpty's last words before he takes a fall and cracks his head. Someone could base a whole book on the rumor—if no one has already.

A GENUINE FOLK TALE

Was this all just the collective fantasy of thousands of Beatle-obsessed imaginations? A year later—by which time almost everyone had been persuaded of Paul's continued existence, but not of the Beatles' own innocence in perpetrating the rumor—John Lennon insisted to *Rolling Stone's* Jann Wenner: "The whole thing was made up. We wouldn't do anything like that. . . . People have nothing better to do than study Bibles and make myths about it, and study rocks and make stories about how people used to live and all that. You know, it's just something to do for them, they live vicariously."

If so, that doesn't necessarily make the saga any less fascinating. That the Beatles cult was capable of spinning an elaborate mythic web without any participation from John, Paul, George, and Ringo indicates how far they had been elevated toward the status of demigods in the imaginations of their disciples. In that sense, the McCartney legend recalls, for example, the film *Yellow Submarine*—but with the difference that the latter was consciously put together by a small, tightly knit group of people. Paul-Is-Dead (whose germ has been traced variously to an Ohio Wesleyan University student's thesis and to a prankish article in an Illinois University student newspaper) was created—or developed— by thousands scattered across America. As such, it can be seen as a genuine folk tale of the mass communications era.

Yet there are many who, despite all the denials, remain convinced that the entire cosmic joke was masterminded by the Beatles themselves. The sheer number of Paul-Is-Dead clues, it is argued, stretches the long arm of coincidence beyond the breaking point. After all, the Beatles were notorious for sly, outrageous stunts—ranging from slipping a falsetto chorus of "tit tit tit" into "Girl" way back in 1965, to the blank L.P. cover and the surprise endings on each side of *Abbey Road*. Why wouldn't they have taken it into their heads to link such pranks into a definite pattern—and in the process perpetrate the most monumental hoax since Orson Welles' *War of the Worlds* broadcast persuaded thousands of panicky New Jerseyites that Martian invaders were in the vicinity? . . .

OUT OF THE PUBLIC EYE

While the rumor snowballed, McCartney remained in Scottish seclusion, going, according to friends, "through heavy changes." During the six months following *Abbey Road* he granted few interviews, and his only audible contribution to the music scene was Badfinger's first hit, "Come and Get It," which he wrote and produced, and which was used as the theme song for the Peter Sellers/Ringo Starr film, *The Magic Christian*.

Starr and Harrison also tended to avoid the public eye, though George did make a low profile return to the concert stage, backing up Delaney and Bonnie. Ringo busied himself with a solo album dedicated to his mother, featuring such "standards" as "Night and Day" and "Love Is a Many-Splendored Thing." ("Get *way* back" went the *Rolling Stone* headline.) Ringo gave Quincy Jones, Richard Perry, Les Reed, Maurice Gibb of the Bee Gees, Paul McCartney, and seven others one song each with which to explore their talents as big band arrangers. But nobody could possibly have brought a more implausible voice to bear on such a project than Mr. Starkey; and when *Sentimental Journey* (originally titled *Ringo Starrdust*) appeared in early 1970, the reaction of critics, fans, and John Lennon was one of embarrassed silence.

Lennon was by far the most visible and prolific Beatle during this period. On September 13 he gave his first major concert in years, at Toronto's huge open-air "rock 'n' roll revival." Only two days beforehand he had received a call from the producers, offering to fly him over at their own expense and reserve him a pair of choice tickets. Lennon's impulsive reply was that he would love to come—but on condition that he and Yoko be allowed to appear on stage with their band, instead of just sitting in the front row "like the King and Queen."

As the Plastic Ono Band was, at that point, still purely conceptual, John persuaded bassist Klaus Voormann, drummer Alan White, and (at the last minute) guitarist Eric Clapton to join forces with him. Then Lennon himself chickened out and missed his plane, before being finally coaxed onto the last possible flight. That, however, ruled out the luxury of a rehearsal; so John kicked off his show with the announcement: "We're just gonna do numbers that we know, y'know, 'cause we've never played together before." The crowd cheered ecstatically at the mere sound of his Liverpool accent, which evidently reassured Lennon, who later said he had been violently ill with a case of nerves just before stepping onto the stage. . . .

JOHN'S NEW PROJECTS

Upon returning to London, John recorded "Cold Turkey" with Clapton, Voormann, and Ringo. The second Plastic Ono Band single left little doubt about the direction Lennon's rock 'n' roll was taking: no frills, no soft-soap—or, as he himself put it—"no bullshit." In "Cold Turkey" the melody—if it can be called that—seldom strays out of a cramped three-note range. The record is too slow for dancing, too raucous for daydreaming. The words are similarly bleak, both in style and in content. . . .

After composing "Cold Turkey," Lennon "went to the other three Beatles and said: 'Hey lads, I think I've written a new single.'" Paul, however, wasn't too sold on the idea. "So I thought: 'Bugger you, I'll put it out myself.'"

For good measure, John refused to credit his harrowing piece to "Lennon-McCartney," effectively ending a 13-year tradition. . . .

On December 15 the Plastic Ono Band performed a UNICEF benefit at London's Lyceum ballroom, augmented with such superstars as Keith Moon, Billy Preston, and Delaney and Bonnie and Friend George Harrison. The program consisted of extended improvisations on only two songs— "Cold Turkey" and "Don't Worry Kyoko"—which Lennon proclaimed "the most fantastic music I've ever heard." (The recordings that surfaced on 1972's *Some Time in New York City* suggest he may have been exaggerating.)

The next day the Lennons landed in Canada for the third time in eight months to announce "a big peace and music festival to be held at Mosport Park near Toronto. We aim to make it the biggest music festival in history, and we're going to ask everyone who's anyone to play . . . and then give a percentage of the gross to a new peace fund. . . .

"Everyone who's into peace," John continued, "will regard the New Year as Year One A.P. (for 'After Peace'). All of our letters and calendars from now on will use this method.

"Along with the festival we are going to have an International Peace Vote. We're asking everyone to vote for either peace or war. When we've got about 20 million votes we're going to give them to the United States.". . .

Shortly after Year One's organizers passed word that the Beatles, Bob Dylan, and a convoy of U.F.O.'s were all likely to appear, in Toronto the coming July, Lennon called the whole thing quits. The reasons given involved business differences, but after Altamont, the rock festival was on its way out anyway. The counterculture had lost one of its most potent symbols; and it was about to lose another.

NOTHING IS FUN ANYMORE

The Beatles' few remaining meetings seldom produced anything but further disagreement. Once, when Paul tried to corral the others into going back on the road, John stunned him with the words: "I want a divorce." Both McCartney and Klein persuaded him to reconsider, or at least not to sound off to the press.

On another occasion, preserved on tape (the Beatles having caught Andy Warhol's habit of letting tape recorders eavesdrop on intimate conversations), John and George presented Paul with an ultimatum. Lennon said he was tired of playing a bit part in "pre-packaged productions," conceived by and tailored to the genius of Paul McCartney. Henceforth the three Beatles must each be awarded precisely four songs per album, with Ringo getting to add one or two if he so desired. Paul complained that that kind of arbitrary regimentation was more suited to the military than to the Beatles, but the others insisted it was the only way to insure a fair shake for all.

That proved to be a moot point, however, as the fabulous foursome never made it back into the recording studio. In the absence of fresh Beatles product (the *Get Back/Let It Be* tapes continued to languish on the shelf) Klein patched ten old singles together to create an L.P. for the American market; his title, *The Beatles Again*, was revised by public demand to *Hey Jude*.

Meanwhile, the *Beatles Monthly*, an institution pre-dating "She Loves You," had bit the dust after 77 issues. Its December 1969 swan song consisted primarily of an editorial harangue against the boys in the band—a harsh coda to the gushy tone the publication had sustained throughout the previous six-and-a-half years. The Beatles were denounced for having grown uncooperative about posing for photographs; for having failed to come out against drugs; for having lost their sense of humor ("Everything seems to be very, very serious. Nothing is just plain fun anymore."); and even for their appearance ("The Beatles are certainly tremendously photogenic, or at least they were in the days when you could see all of their faces.").

The main reason for the folding, however, was that rock's greatest partnership was itself on the rocks. But it was not until April 9, 1970, that Paul McCartney—of all people—made that official.

CHAPTER 5

LEGACY

The Longest Lasting Music Hall Performance

Charles Paul Freund

Acknowledging a resurgence of Beatlemania in the twenty-first century, Charles Paul Freund, a senior editor of *Reason* magazine, dissects the Beatles' popularity both during the sixties and in the new century. In the following article, Freund argues against the notion that the Beatles were rock-and-roll revolutionaries. Freund insists that the original hits of the Beatles were within the well-established pop formula and that their later experiments were outgrowths of this pop foundation. Freund concludes that rock music embraced the Beatles' pop music sensibilities and incorporated them into the everchanging definition of rock and roll.

The catchy pop styling of the Beatles may help explain their endurance, but fans were also tuned into the mature storytelling of the band's lyrics and their evocation of older forms of music and showmanship that trace back to nineteenth-century British Music Hall traditions. To Freund, these elements—which transcend specific cultural contexts that would otherwise date the music—made it easy for later generations to appreciate the Beatles' songs and remake them to fit their own desires or needs.

Is anything more intricately intertwined with its time than the career of the Beatles? According to the usual account, the group's shifting personae, from the original 1964 mania through the 1970 break-up, either led or reflected the period's changing tastes and behavior. For Americans of a certain age, it was seven delirious years of teenybopper screaming, androgynous hair-doing, cartoon-India meditating, psychedelic drug taking, syncretic sitar strumming, and all-you-need-is-loving.

Is that wrong? Surely not. If the increasingly brittle idea of "the '60s" has any meaning aside from common nostalgia, it describes the transformation of a type of cultural fandom into a type of social and political identity. The Beatles managed to remain at the center of this phenomenon—if not ahead of it—as long as they existed. Their fans, primarily leading-edge boomers, became what they beheld. Which of them is not part Beatle?

Now another transformation is underway. Older boomers are starting to retire, enrolling in the AARP, and leafing uneasily through its *Modern Maturity* magazine. It may have helped their transition when [in 2000] Sir Paul McCartney appeared on *Modern Maturity*'s cover, with an interview inside about the losses, the challenges, and even the pleasures of growing older. Another boomer milestone, another Beatles persona. Nor is that the final such crossroads: Such Beatles songs as "In My Life" seem to be cued up regularly at boomer memorials.

BEATLEMANIA AGAIN

So how is it that this year [2001], *Rolling Stone* used its cover to proclaim the Beatles as the "World's Hottest Band"? Since the release last November of *1*, that compilation of 27 No. 1 Beatles hits has been selling at a pace that could make it the biggest-selling CD ever. How is it that a huge $60 volume called *The Beatles Anthology*, featuring old interviews and writings, is setting new sales standards for the coffee-table tome? The black-and-white Beatles movie, *A Hard Day's Night*, has been back in theatrical release. Beatles hit singles are getting increased rotation even in radio contexts where they were sparingly played, such as on classic-rock album formats. A Beatles cookbook has somehow appeared (*She Came in Through the Kitchen Window*), and so has the Beatles' "first and only official Web site," thebeatles.com. Even some out-of-print Beatles books are back, including a volume of post-Beatles interviews with John Lennon, then in his Lord Byron wannabe stage, in which he expresses his utter contempt for the Beatles.

The new Beatlemania has surprised many people, especially because so many buyers of the new CD are under 20. That means that many new Beatles fans were born after

John Lennon's 1980 murder. What can the Beatles mean to such listeners? Why such persistence? Certainly the older boomers don't get it. As *The New York Times* put it—in a headline, yet—last January [2000]: "The Beatles Never Die, But Why? Ask Fans."

Some newspaper accounts have quoted pleased older boomers, who "explain" that these songs have "stood the test of time." But that merely reposes the original question: Why did they stand this supposed test? Some journalists have pointed to Capitol Records' heavy promotion of the CD on kid-oriented cable channel Nickelodeon, which has pushed the CD toward a young audience. That has probably helped sustain sales, but it doesn't address why young viewers have embraced music twice as old as they are. Anyway, since when do teen consumers identify with music that is so closely associated with a previous generation? Isn't teen culture usually about distancing a rising generation from its predecessors?

Besides, to focus on such factors as promotion is to fall into the usual "pop culture" trap. According to this common view, phenomena such as the original Beatlemania are best understood as events cynically engineered by the culture industries. "Mass" forms such as music, movies, TV shows, and the like are thus supposedly fashioned according to market research and sold to gullible consumers. Cultural industrialists may well wish they had this power, but they obviously don't. They can only try to guess, after the fact, why some of their artifacts succeed and others fail. Accumulated market research notwithstanding, there is neither pop culture nor mass culture; in the end there is only personal culture. Each consumer uses cultural artifacts, the Beatles included, according to his or her peculiar and usually shifting needs.

THE BEATLES AND THE NEW GENERATION

To ask "Why?" about this Beatles resurgence is to pose the wrong question. A better question is "Who?" As in, Who are the Beatles now? While each new fan will probably answer that question differently, 21st-century fans are certainly using the group and its music differently from the original fans of the 1960s. That is, the meanings that boomers attribute to the Beatles are no longer the group's only meanings. Alternative hearings of the familiar songs have emerged, and these are claiming their own validity. Some new fans may be hearing the CD through the groups and music that have come since, in terms of musical influence. Some may be hearing the songs historically, attempting to associate it with their own understanding of the 1960s. Some may be using the music to distance themselves from their own contemporaries.

Leading-edge boomers engaged in the same sort of cultural appropriation: When they flocked to Humphrey Bogart film festivals in the 1960s, they used his character and films for their own purposes, which were no doubt different from the purposes of the films' original Depression-era audiences. Now they are on the receiving end of the same process.

But there's another nagging question raised by the new Beatlemania. Not just who are the Beatles now, but who were they then? New fans may be using the group for their own purposes, but then so did the original generation of fans. The years since the group's breakup have seen a lot of myth-making and obscuring, in order to fit them better into a pliable narrative of the era and its aftermath. It is worth pausing to listen to the group anew in the context of their own time, because there are some lost chords in their music waiting to sound again.

THE BEATLES IN THE SIXTIES

The Beatles—image, music, and text—are obviously bound up with 1960s teen life, taste, and mentality, and from this vantage point that seems both natural and inevitable. But was it? The fact is, the American teenage audience that lost its head over the Beatles was the group's second American audience. The foursome entered American culture through a different portal: They came in through the MOR window.

It is well-known that American record executives originally regarded the Beatles with complete indifference. The label with the American rights to the group was Capitol, and it refused to release any Beatles records. A notorious 1963 Capitol memo that curtly dismisses the group ("We don't think the Beatles will do anything in this market") is now regarded as a prime instance of bovine corporate stupidity. But Capitol actually had some evidence to support its dim view of the group's U.S. prospects. It could have cited three specific reasons to ignore the Beatles.

Those three reasons were "Please Please Me," "From Me to You," and "She Loves You." While Capitol originally wasn't interested in these songs, some smaller U.S. labels were willing to take a chance with them. All three of these

records were released in the U.S. market in 1963, two by
Vee-Jay and one by Swan, albeit with minimal promotion.
What happened? Nobody played them. "From Me to You" did
chart on the long Billboard list at No. 116, but neither "Please
Please Me" nor "She Loves You" charted at all.

Late in the year, however, a Washington, D.C., disc jockey
named Carroll James ("CJ the DJ"), started to play the
British pressing of "I Want to Hold Your Hand." James had a
girlfriend who worked for a British airline; she had observed
British Beatlemania firsthand, and brought back the group's
latest 45. The Washington audience loved the song. Capitol
noticed. The big label had already agreed to a limited U.S.
release of the record, with an unambitious pressing that reflected the label's low hopes and lack of interest. Now, Capitol considered releasing it quickly in the Washington area.

But someone at James' station had already sent a tape of
"I Want to Hold Your Hand" to a DJ friend in Chicago, who
started playing it, too; Chicago soon sent it to St. Louis. Capitol decided to press a million copies of the record immediately, and to promote the group hard. The rest is hysteria.

Except for the details: Carroll James wasn't a rock DJ, and
his audience was mostly grown-ups. James did a talky afternoon drive-time show for WWDC, a popular AM station. Back
then, WWDC was a laid-back outlet with a so-called "middle
of the road," or MOR, format that was aimed at an older audience. What did it do besides break the Beatles? When it wasn't
running its oddball contests, the station drew on a mostly pop
play list, mixing Andy Williams and Al Hirt with soft-rock acts
like Ruby and the Romantics, Bobby Vinton, and Ben E. King.
WWDC's morning guy had been around for decades, played
the organ behind his own wake-up patter, and had a pair of
miked, twittering canaries in the studio with him. At night,
WWDC didn't play any music at all; it interviewed touring
book authors. The only show it aimed at a young audience
was in the evening, when its preferred adult listeners were
watching TV, and that show was targeted at the dutiful children of the station's core middle-class following. The "teen"
show was called The House of Homework, and its gimmick
was letting kids call in to ask for help with their assignments.

PURVEYORS OF POP

In short, WWDC was a station for dorks. Nobody who aimed
for Hip or Cool would have listened to it. Carroll James him-

self used to play snippets of Bob Dylan's early records as jokes, in disbelief that the folkie actually existed. On the other hand, every single program director at every hip, cool rock station in America had already thrown his copies of "Please Please Me" and "She Loves You" into the trash. One dorky Washington station played the Beatles for an audience of commuting office workers, at-home moms, and their bookish kids—and they wanted more. How could this be? Who could the Beatles have been to these listeners?

In fact, the MOR audience had a template for receiving the Beatles that nobody else had, because MOR stations were the only part of the American music scene at all open to British vocal acts. Top 40 rock listeners accepted foreign singers only as sideshow displays; Lonnie Donegan's 1961 novelty "Does Your Chewing Gum Lose Its Flavor?" was a Top 10 hit. But, unlike rock listeners, the MOR audience was familiar with Britain's biggest pre-Beatles singer, Cliff Richard, who was one of the most popular acts in the world. Richard and his band, later famous as the Shadows, had had a middling 1959 hit here called "Living Doll," and Richard was getting some MOR airplay in 1963 with "Lucky Lips." (He would finally get a Top 10 U.S. hit—"Devil Woman"—in 1976.) MOR stations had featured a string of mostly minor hits by British singers, including Frank Ifield ("I Remember You"), Helen Shapiro ("Tell Me What He Said"), and Matt Munro ("My Kind of Girl"). These were largely treacly, '50s-style pop records: Munro had a lounge-crooner sound; Shapiro was a Connie Francis–style torch singer. What did the Beatles have in common with acts like these?

Quite a bit, actually. The early Beatles sang Ifield's hits in their live shows, and toured with Helen Shapiro. (Indeed, "She Loves You" could well be an answer record—then a genre of its own—to Shapiro's musically inventive "Tell Me What He Said.") While boomers may cherish the image of the early Beatles as leather-clad bad boys playing raw rock in smoky Hamburg clubs, the reality is that along with the rock covers, their Hamburg repertoire also included lots of sappy old pop standards like "Red Sails in the Sunset." The mammoth *Meet the Beatles* album, after all, features a version of Anita Bryant's syrupy "'Til There Was You." Perhaps the greatest tribute to the intensity of the original U.S. Beatlemania is that even this intolerable piece of anti-rock made the era's Top 40 playlists.

POP PERSISTENCE

So what? Given the Beatles' long career, their dozens of hits, and their various notable innovations, what possible significance can their early, brief connection to a pop audience have? In fact, it is in the context of their career that it matters, because the group's pop dimension is a key factor not only in their musical "growth," but in the longevity of their music as well.

Although Beatles' music is currently fixed in the musical canon as having revolutionized rock, that is not quite correct. What is true is that the group's enormous success opened the door to a lot of groups who energized the era's rock playlists, though even this element can be—and has been—vastly overstated. Early '60s rock was far from being the string-laden wasteland it is sometimes made out to have been (think of the Crystals' "Da Do Ron Ron," for instance). It is also true that the Beatles made long-form compositions possible, introduced the concept album, and, through their lyrics, helped bring personal expression into a field that was largely formulaic. However, the Beatles are themselves indebted to others for some of these advances (among them, Bob Dylan and Paul Simon). Besides, these later changes often occurred at the cost of the very musical energy that the Beatles are otherwise credited with restoring to the rock scene.

But is the Beatles' own career and development really a study in rock revolution, as it is usually portrayed? Or is it actually something different: a study in the extension of the otherwise despised pop form? The answer to that question could help resolve the apparent mysteries of the group's persistence. Here's the short answer: The mature Beatles, the Beatles who "revolutionized" rock music from *Revolver* through *Sgt. Pepper's Lonely Hearts Club Band* through the end of their common career, the Beatles who helped construct the foundation of the '60s counterculture, were themselves built on an essentially pop foundation and enjoyed an essentially pop fluorescence.

By 1966, the Beatles were far more interested in melody than in beat, had largely abandoned the influences from American country music and American blues that had been apparent on their earlier recordings, and were building an increasing number of their compositions around narrative lyrics that told stories rather than expressed adolescent emotions. The more they developed as composers and lyricists, the less they tried to harmonize like the Everly Brothers or whoop like the Isley Brothers, and the more they drew on their own roots in British popular music. While they continued to use rock elements to make their music, there is almost as much British Music Hall in their later work as there is rock.

The apotheosis of their personal development is not the avant-garde experimentation of the White Album (only a few of its cuts get much play anymore). It is *Abbey Road,* which, dear as it is to the hearts of many rock enthusiasts, could just as well be hailed as the greatest pop album of all time. Certainly, it could have been played almost in its entirety on MOR radio. As for the Beatles' career coda, the *Let It Be* album, its major songs—especially the title number and the whining "Long and Winding Road"—out-treacle anything that Matt Munro ever dared record.

ROCK AND POP

Does this distinction between "pop" and "rock" actually matter? From the point of view of the music, no. One either likes the stuff or doesn't. But from the vantage point of rock mythology, the distinction is potentially revealing.

Over the years, what might be called the rock establishment—the music's historians, its journalists, often its performers, and now a class of academics, too—has developed a complex story of the music's origins, nature, and social role. As humanities professor Robert Pattison has pointed out, this story has been laid out along the lines of 19th-century Romanticism. Unlike other forms of music, goes the myth, rock prides itself on being elemental. Though it was commercialized by whites, its soul is black. Its true roots are in Africa by way of the Mississippi Delta. Stolen from blacks by Sun Records in the guise of Elvis Presley, the music nevertheless remains true to its undeniable nature. It is a music that stands outside middle-class restraint, reveling in its sexual power, emerging from—and this is a real phrase from a real musicologist—"orgiastic magic." Some statement of primitivist obligation is essential to the pose of rock seriousness, and it is in fact part of the Beatles' persona as well.

No grand narrative is complete without a vanquished villain, and this narrative features one, too: pop music. Pop was everything rock hated. Pop was polite; rock is outspoken. Pop was false; rock is authentic. Pop was constrained; rock lets it all hang out. Pop was commercial artifice; rock is, in Pattison's portrait, Walt Whitman's "barbaric yawp," updated and indispensable to surviving a corrupt consumerist world.

Not much of this story has any merit. Rock music is obviously indebted to black forms that preceded it, but these forms aren't African. The various kinds of black music that developed here are American, and were themselves influenced by other American forms. Efforts by such music writers as Gerald Early to demonstrate the indebtedness of Sam Cooke, Marvin Gaye, and other '60s black crooners to an Italian-American model (an overtly pop model) have yet to be absorbed into this myth. There's no Romantic capital in that story. Similarly, rock is indebted to the "country" musical forms that emerged from a variety of influences, including European yodels, but there's not much Romantic capital in saying that, either.

But the real problem with this myth is its treatment of pop. Rock describes not one type of music, but a variety of styles that have influenced each other, including doo-wop harmonizing, boogie-woogie, jump forms of swing, soul music, rockabilly, etc. Looming over the other influences, however, is none other than pop.

The pop music of the '50s that was overwhelmed by rock was the last stage of big-band music; band singers like Perry Como and Rosemary Clooney displaced the bands as headline attractions after World War II, though they continued to perform in the old-fashioned idiom of the band era. While rock swept many of these singers offstage, the younger vocalists who replaced them quickly took up the same traditional pop narrative that has been going on since the 1890s, when the first commercial hit song ("After the Ball") established it. That narrative addresses a limited number of themes involving social identity, pleasure, personal fulfillment, and, above all, issues of courtship. These themes continued to dominate the new rock charts as they had the earlier songs, even though they were sung, played, and received in new ways. The musical break in the 1950s was not one of emotional substance, as the rock establishment likes to suggest; it was one of emotional style.

ROCK IN DECAY

The separation between these two emotional styles is not nearly so distinct as rock would like to think. While rock is never threatened by its other influences—it is never about to become the blues, much less jump or country music—it has repeatedly been threatened by pop.

In fact, one of the original merits of the Beatles is, supposedly, that they arrived to rescue American rock at just such a point of decay. According to this take, Elvis had been reduced to a bel-canto fraud, singing such horrors as a rewrite of "O Sole Mio" ("It's Now or Never"); acts such as Ben E. King were doing over-lush numbers like "Spanish Harlem" and "Amor"; pop figures such as Steve Lawrence and Eydie Gorme had been sneaking back into the Top 10; the Beach Boys were doing barbershop harmonies; the model of teen excitement was Rick Nelson, a sitcom spinoff. Rock was forgetting itself amid symphonic arrangements and a crooner revival, when suddenly the Beatles exploded on the scene with three guitars, a set of drums, a bluesy harmonica, and a "Whoa, yeah!" whoop.

This is a tendentious picture of the time; it ignores, among other matters, James Brown, early Motown, Phil Spector, and the Atlantic Records groups (such as the Drifters), and it downplays the merits of Brill Building music. But it's not an entirely false picture, either. The Beatles, along with the torrent of British Invasion groups that followed them into the American market, trimmed the Top 40's excrescences, invigorated its sound, and addressed its audience with new subjects.

This story is often interpreted in terms of rock's Romantic myth. According to this narrative, British musicians had been closer students of America's own musical heritage than Americans had been, especially regarding the lost heritage of the blues. British groups listened eagerly to recordings that most Americans didn't know existed, incorporated the rhythms and instrumentation into their own styles, and returned the vigorous result to surprised and delighted American audiences. This story is demonstrably true for many of the British (and Irish) groups that enjoyed American success; one can clearly hear the influence in the early hits of such groups as the Animals, the Yardbirds, Them, the Spencer Davis Group, and, obviously, the Rolling Stones.

This story is applicable, at least in part, to the Beatles as well. For two years after their explosion into the American market, the Beatles released a long series of singles and albums in the American style. Their own compositions and their choice of cover versions reflected their enthusiasm for the music of such U.S. artists as Chuck Berry and Little Richard, and their willing adherence to the familiar pop themes of courtship and fulfillment. This was the "early Beatles" period of making music to dance and cruise to. It seems to be the preferred Beatles period for many leading-edge boomers, perhaps because, as radio and party music that was used socially, it's evocative of their adolescence.

But this is not the music that has shaped the Beatles' later reputation. If the group's career had ended in 1965, it would probably be remembered—with as much embarrassment as pleasure—for the intense mania it inspired, and only secondarily for the songs. Although it's largely forgotten now, a Beatles backlash was gaining steam by the time *Rubber Soul* was released in 1965. The group's cherubic cheerfulness was beginning to seem flabby compared to other groups' tougher material. Yet the Beatles today occupy a uniquely transcendent position in the rock world, and a reputation for innovative genius. How did they achieve this? By turning down rock's volume.

A New Path for Rock

With the release of *Revolver* in 1966, the Beatles began to transform themselves from teen idols into storytellers. Throughout the album, they display a genuine talent for creating characters, states of mind, and dramatic situations, and for doing so by suggestion and with the use of spare images. In other words, the album invited not only a rock listening, but a literary listening. The outstanding example is "Eleanor Rigby," a Bronte novel in miniature, unrecognizable as a rock number. But songs like "For No One," "She Said, She Said," "And Your Bird Can Sing," and "Tomorrow Never Knows" are all departures from the rock idiom, offering unusual imagery, surprising allusions, and verbal riddles. Most of the cuts are heavily melodic and carefully arranged. One of the album's chart hits, the sing-song "Yellow Submarine," reaches back beyond rock for its inspiration. A children's song, it pointed in the direction the Beatles were to go: the British Music Hall.

Sgt. Pepper's (1967) may well have transformed the rock world, but it owes nothing to rock's Romantic myth. It is built largely from the music and imagery of the Victorian and Edwardian pleasure palaces of the industrial working class. (Herman's Hermits had already revived the Music Hall standard, "I'm Henry VIII, I Am," but as a 1965 novelty song.) Though the Beatles approached the material with a literary sensibility, especially irony, songs like "When I'm 64" and "Lovely Rita" are effective evocations of antique Music Hall style, while "Getting Better" and the melodramatic "She's Leaving Home" make sympathetic use of antique emotion. Indeed, the corny, melodic sentimentalism of the Music Hall repertoire was a rich vein for the group, and they were never to abandon it.

A long list of later Beatles songs is drawn, directly or indirectly, from this tradition: "Martha, My Dear," "Your Mother Should Know," "Penny Lane," "All You Need Is Love," "All Together Now," "Ob-La-Di, Ob-La-Da," "Honey Pie," "Maxwell's Silver Hammer," "Magical Mystery Tour," "Good Night," and almost everything on the B side of *Abbey Road*, down to and including the inner-groove run-out, "Her Majesty." While the Beatles continued to write and record rock songs such as "Revolution" and "Come Together," and while they engaged in some entirely different musical experiments on the White Album, the influences that shaped their major, later output—most of the music for which they are best known—emerges from an antique pop style.

These two elements of the Beatles' career—their development as narrators, and their exploitation of Music Hall content and style—lift the group's music into a context of its own. It is these elements that are able to claim the attention of an audience that was born long after the group broke up. But what do either of these elements have to do with the mythology that the rock establishment embraces? Precious little. In the end, the rock world's head was turned by music that was sweet, corny, artificial, and intensely sentimental. Rock has yet to come to grips with this.

WHAT IS OLD IS NEW

"Their music doesn't grow old," according to Beetles authority Bill Harry, compiler of the 720-page *Ultimate Beatles Encyclopedia*. Actually, much of it is drawn from musical conventions that were so old that the group's American following didn't know them. Fans were free to create their own context for the music, and to create their own associations and meanings. That the music's sensibilities arrived from such sources as Paul McCartney's musician father didn't matter decades ago, and certainly doesn't matter now.

"A lot of my musicality came from my dad," says McCartney in the new Beatles coffee-table book. He cherishes his boyhood memories of lying on the rug while his father played the piano and explained the "clever" parts of the old songs he once performed. According to Paul, such memories are why he is "so open about sentimentality."

The Beatles' 21st century fans are already assembling their own memories of the group, choosing among Beatles "eras," and even asserting their primacy. One of them recently told *USA Today* that "In some ways, we are more sincere fans in that, unlike the baby boomers who see The Beatles as a form of nostalgia, we pick The Beatles over all the music of today and make a conscious choice to experience a group of 35 years ago."

"We hope you all will sing along," sang the Beatles in "Sgt. Pepper's." In fact, singing along, pint in hand, was a staple of the 19th century Music Hall experience. In a sense, everybody did sing along, and more fans than ever seem to be joining in. Many of the original boomers thought at the time that the Beatles were helping raise the roof of a new culture. If so, they did it by opening the longest lasting Music Hall performance of all time, entertaining, infectious, and dripping with sentiment down to the last note.

The Beatles as Cultural Artifact

Kevin Michael Grace

Kevin Michael Grace, the former senior editor at the *Report* newsmagazine (a now-defunct Canadian journal), argues that because of endless revisiting of the Beatles' careers and music, the band has become more of a phenomenon that is divorced from its cultural roots. According to Grace, this seems to jibe well with a newer generation of listeners who have no attachment to the sixties, let alone more recent events. But Grace acknowledges that there is something timeless in the Beatles' music that connects on some level with later generations. This element—supported by continuing critical interest—has left the band a cultural artifact similar to the canon of great books or enduring works of art.

In a March 4, 1966, interview with Maureen Cleave of the *London Evening Standard*, John Lennon declared, "Christianity will go. It will vanish and shrink. I needn't argue with that; I'm right and will be proved right. We're more popular than Jesus now. I don't know which will go first—rock and roll or Christianity." Thirty-four years later, John Lennon is 20 years dead. Christianity is rather more popular than Lennon would have liked; but the Beatles are rather more popular than he could have imagined.

They released their last album in 1970, the year John, Paul, George and Ringo went their separate ways. Last month [in November 2000] their record company released *1*, a compilation of all their No. 1 hits—from the insipid "Love Me Do," to the lugubrious "The Long and Winding Road," with 25 rather better songs in between—on one CD. It went straight to No. 1 in Canada, the U.S. and Britain, an achievement unprecedented in the history of popular music. The album has quickly become the fastest selling record of all time.

ENDLESSLY REPACKAGING

"Does it really need an explanation?" asks Ira Robbins, editor of the *Trouser Press Record Guide*. "Not to be dismissive, but this is essentially a marketing moment. It's not as if people are suddenly rising up and saying, 'God, those Beatles were really great!' We've just seen Lennon's 60th birthday, the 20th anniversary of his death, the Rock and Roll Hall of Fame Exhibit, the miniseries. It's just one of those years that's going to be good for the Beatles."

And there's *The Beatles Anthology*, a coffee-table compilation of pictures and interviews heavy enough to kill a cat, that lists at $92 and sits at No. 1 on the *Washington Post*'s General/Non-fiction best-sellers list. Two weeks ago [in December 2000], *Rolling Stone* declared "Yesterday" the greatest pop song of all time, while in August, *Mojo* declared "In My Life" the greatest song of all time. In June, *Q* opined that *Revolver* was the greatest British album ever.

Yet none of this explains why *1* went to No. 1. It does offer better value for money than other Beatles compilations, but these songs have been endlessly repackaged, and there are no rarities or other extras. So who's buying it? Jay, a clerk at the downtown Vancouver Sam The Record Man, reports that about half his store's sales are to the middle-aged.

A REFLECTION OF A GENERATION

For the boomers, the Beatles need no explanation. Oldies radio stations claim they play the "soundtrack of your lives," but for the '60s generation, the Beatles were more than just the soundtrack. It is hard to explain to younger people just how ubiquitous they were. There had never been a phenomenon like Beatlemania, and there never will be again. The Beatles were the standard-bearer for a youth movement that was beginning to feel its power and would soon bring governments to their knees. Lennon apologized, in typically sarcastic fashion, for his outburst to Maureen Cleave, but what he said was arguably true. His blasphemy made the front page of every newspaper in the non-Communist world.

But it was impossible to stay angry with them for long. Young people dressed like them, talked like them, wore their hair and beards like them, took drugs because they did and adopted Eastern spirituality because they took a short-lived liking to a "giggling guru" called the Maharishi. Eat your heart out, Slim Shady [rapper Eminem].

PART OF THE FUTURE, NOT PART OF THE PAST

Devin McKinney was only four years old when the Beatles broke up. His introduction to them as well as an overidealized sense of the 1960s was therefore derived from secondhand experience. In the following selection from the end of his biography of the Beatles and their times, McKinney comes to the realization that his sentimental longing to have been part of the sixties was really a desire to escape his current responsibilities. The lesson McKinney learns is that to live his life in an imagined past would be to surrender his own concept of the Beatles that could only have been developed through his modern-day sensibilities as well as historical hindsight.

I had always coveted the direct experiences, earned wisdoms, and epochal blessings bestowed on the '60s veterans. At any point in my growing up, I felt I would have given all I had to trade places with the merest and most marginal of them. What I had never realized or appreciated until now—alone in a cramped Manhattan room, suddenly pushing thirty—was that trading places in the historical line would have meant giving up the precise set of psychological biases, intellectual limitations, aesthetic prejudices, and personal experiences that had shaped me into the possessor of a relationship with the Beatles and the '60s unique from that of anyone who had ever given thought to either.

What had been my sweetest and bitterest fantasy was now almost horrifying. Without this identity, after all, I would never have been able to twist the Beatles into the many private shapes I had asked them to assume. Never have been able to construct, through an interpretation of dream and study of history, my own version of the story they had once imagined and enacted. Change an instant of my experience, and the Beatles—*my* Beatles, my customized version of their meanings and metaphysics—would be stolen from me.

That decided it. What I could say, at last, was that I would *not* trade my place in history, whatever this place was or wasn't, for any other. . . .

I had finally taken my highest cue from the Beatles and decided to live my life as if it were not predetermined but yet to be made, neither craving nor cursing another's past. I was whatever I was. I would never experience the '60s, and my time would likely never see such extremes. The '60s would never be a part of my past, but some of their soul could remain a part of my present, and my future—unavoidably, unforeseeably, thrillingly—would be *something else.*

Devin McKinney, *Magic Circles: The Beatles in Dream and History.* Cambridge, MA: Harvard University Press, 2003.

Langdon Winner wrote that with the 1967 release of *Sgt. Pepper* the Western world was more unified than it had been since the Congress of Vienna in 1815. It sounds fatuous today, but it was true. Tony Palmer was ridiculed for comparing the Beatles' songs to Schubert's compositions, but it is doubtful that the great poets Schubert set to music—even Goethe—moved youth as intensely as Lennon and McCartney did.

Enthusiasts even claimed the Beatles were the Beethovens of their day. Thirty years—even 130 years—after his death, people listened to Beethoven's works with greater enthusiasm than they had when he was alive. Brahms despaired of writing symphonies because it was believed that Ludwig van had exhausted the genre. Nobody has ever claimed that the Fab Four exhausted the pop song.

A CULTURAL ARTIFACT

So what do today's youth see in the Beatles? Rachel Sa, a 19-year-old Sun Media columnist and University of Toronto undergraduate, says, "They are really huge at my university." In her opinion, "If music or any kind of popular culture can transcend a generation, it's going to survive." She confesses, "I'm not an avid fan, but I do enjoy their music." She prefers David Bowie, who became a star in the 1970s. Coincidentally, Bowie has recently been named the most influential living musician by the *New Musical Express.* Radiohead was second, the Beatles third.

When asked to give a visual image of the 1960s, Ms. Sa chooses the movie *Woodstock.* She has never known an unsegregated musical world. "When I was in school the teeny-boppers listened to New Kids On The Block; now they listen to Ricky Martin and Britney Spears," she says. "They're huge now, but will they last? God, I hope not."

Editor Robbins says the recrudescent popularity of the Beatles is "one of the very rare cases in recent years where you've seen cultural memory actually extend backwards. Bands that were exciting to us in our 30s [he is 45] are not even on the radar screen for people aged 15. Young people today grow up fully capable of denying that anything they didn't live through didn't happen. You watch VH1's *Behind The Music,* and all the stuff that happened more than five or 10 years ago is comical to young people. Charlie Chaplin, the Beatles and the Clash are pretty much equivalently in the distant past."

When asked earlier this year what his favourite album was, Al Gore picked *Revolver*. But then, as Mr. Robbins points out, Mr. Gore also claimed his favourite novel is Stendhal's *The Red and the Black*. Mr. Robbins concludes, "The Beatles fit in a box called 'Greatest Band.'" Here is the secret of their continuing success: they have become a cultural artifact, Jane Austen with yeah, yeah, yeahs. John Lennon would not have liked that. So maybe Christianity has won after all.

APPENDIX OF DOCUMENTS

DOCUMENT 1: COCKY IN HAMBURG

John Lennon recounts how "making show" in the Hamburg club scene in 1960 differed from the early Beatles' performances in the United Kingdom.

We'd done the Johnny Gentle tour, but we'd only been on stage a bit, for twenty minutes or so, because he'd be on most of the time. In Liverpool we just used to do our best numbers, the same ones at every gig. In Hamburg we would play for eight hours, so we really had to find new ways of playing. It was still rather thrilling when you went on stage. It was a little nightclub and it was a bit frightening because it wasn't a dance hall, and all these people were sitting down, expecting something.

At first we got a pretty cool reception. The second night the manager told us: 'You were terrible, you have to make a show—"mach shau",' like the group down the road were doing. And of course whenever there was any pressure point I had to get us out of it. The guys said, 'Well, OK John, you're the leader.' When nothing was going on, they'd say, 'Uh-uh, no leader, f— it,' but if anything happened, it was like, 'You're the leader, you get up and do a show.'

We were scared by it all at first, being in the middle of the tough clubland. But we felt cocky, being from Liverpool, at least believing the myth about Liverpool producing cocky people. So I put my guitar down and I did Gene Vincent all night: banging and lying on the floor and throwing the mike about and pretending I had a bad leg. That was some experience. We all did 'mach shauing' all the time from then on.

The Beatles, *The Beatles Anthology.* San Francisco: Chronicle, 2000.

DOCUMENT 2: US TRYING TO DO THE BLUES

In August 1962, "Love Me Do" was recorded at Abbey Road Studios in London. Paul McCartney and John Lennon remember the song's inception, little knowing then that it would become the band's first hit single.

PAUL: "'Love Me Do' was us trying to do the blues. It came out whiter because it always does. We're white and we were just young Liverpool musicians. We didn't have any finesse to be able to actually sound black, but 'Love Me Do' was probably the first bluesy thing we tried to do."

JOHN: "Paul started writing that when he was about 15 and we finished it off over the years. It was the first one that we'd dare do of our own. We were doing such great numbers of other people and then we started to introduce numbers of our own. It was a traumatic experience because we were doing numbers by Ray Charles, Little Richard, and it was a kind of hard thing to suddenly start singing 'Love Me Do'. We all thought that our numbers were a bit wet, you know."

Keith Badman, *The Beatles Off the Record: Outrageous Opinions and Unrehearsed Interviews.* London: Omnibus Press, 2000.

DOCUMENT 5: PETE BEST RECALLS HIS SACKING

Pete Best remembers what an unexpected shock it was on August 16, 1962, when the Beatles' manager, Brian Epstein, told him that he was to be permanently replaced by Ringo Starr. Perhaps the most troubling aspect of his sacking, Best states, was that none of the other band members had had the courage to deliver the bad news.

I found Brian in a very uneasy mood when I joined him in his upstairs office. He came out with a lot of pleasantries and talked anything but business, which was unlike him. These were obviously delaying tactics and something important, I knew, was on his mind. Then he mustered enough courage to drop the bombshell.

'The boys want you out and Ringo in. . . . '

I was stunned and found words difficult. Only one echoed through my mind. Why, why, why?

'They don't think you're a good enough drummer, Pete,' Brian went on. 'And George Martin doesn't think you're a good enough drummer.'

'I consider myself as good, if not better, than Ringo,' I could hear myself saying. Then I asked: 'Does Ringo know about this yet?'

'He's joining on Saturday,' Eppy said.

So everything was all neatly packaged. A conspiracy had clearly been going on for some time behind my back, but not one of the other Beatles could find the courage to tell me. The stab in the back had been left to Brian, and it had been left until almost the last minute. Even Ringo had been a party to it, someone else I had considered to be a pal until this momentous day. He and I had kept our friendship rolling whenever possible since that first trip to Hamburg. We would often meet at lunchtime at the Cavern, where musicians tended to congregate whether they were appearing there or not. We would meet at other venues on the same bill and, of course, at my home if Rory Storm was playing the Casbah.

Epstein went on to what for him was simply next business at this shattering meeting. 'There are still a couple of venues left before Ringo joins—will you play?'

'Yes,' I nodded, not really knowing what I was saying, for my mind was in a turmoil. How could this happen to me? Why had it taken two years for John Lennon, Paul McCartney and George Harrison to decide that my drumming was not of a high enough standard for them? Dazed, I made my way out of Brian's office. Downstairs, Neil was waiting for me. 'What's happened?' he asked as soon as he saw me, 'you look as if you've seen a ghost.'

'They've kicked me out!' I said.

Neil could scarcely believe it either. We headed for the Grapes to sink a couple of pints. 'All I want to do is try to get my thoughts together,' I told him. He was really upset and as disgusted as I was at this sudden, stupefying blow. He began to talk about quitting his job as road manager.

'There's no need for that,' I told him. 'Don't be a fool—the Beatles are going places.'

Pete Best and Patrick Doncaster, *Beatle!: The Pete Best Story*. London: Plexus, 2001.

DOCUMENT 4: THE BEATLES CHARM AMERICA

After they touched down at Kennedy Airport on February 7, 1964, the Beatles gave a press conference. Various questions were hurled at the band, but nothing seemed to faze them. The Beatles' glib and witty responses became part of their innocuous and fun-loving charm.

REPORTER: Are you all bald under those wigs?

JOHN LENNON: I'm bald.

GEORGE HARRISON: And deaf and dumb, too!

JOHN: We're all bald, yes.

REPORTER: What do you think your music does for these people?

PAUL McCARTNEY: Ah, well.

RINGO STARR: Pleases them, I think.

GEORGE: It must do, 'cause they're buying the records.

REPORTER: Have you heard about the "Stamp Out the Beatles" campaign in Detroit?

PAUL: First off, we're bringing out the "Stamp Out Detroit" campaign.

REPORTER: Seriously, what are you going to do about it?

PAUL: About what?

RINGO: How big are they?

REPORTER: Why does it excite them so much?

PAUL: We don't know, really.

JOHN: If we knew, we'd form another group and become managers.

REPORTER: Someone says you guys are nothing but a bunch of British Elvis Presleys.

JOHN: He must be blind.

RINGO: [mocking Elvis's gestures] It's not true. It's not true.

REPORTER: Are you in favor of the lunacy you create?

JOHN: No, it's great fun. We like lunatics. It's healthy.

REPORTER: Would you sing a song?

BEATLES: No!

JOHN: We need money first.

REPORTER: How much money do you intend to take out of America?

JOHN: About a half a crown, two dollars. It depends on the tax.

REPORTER: Do you ever get haircuts?

GEORGE: I had one yesterday. [He laughs.]

RINGO: That's no lie.

GEORGE: Honest, that's the truth.

REPORTER: I think he missed.

GEORGE: No, he didn't.

RINGO: You should have seen him the day before.

REPORTER: Why do you sing like Americans but speak with English accents?

PAUL: That is English, actually.

GEORGE: It's not English. It's Liverpudlian, yah see!

PAUL: The Liverpool accent. The way you say some of the words. You say *grass* instead of saying *graaaasss*. So the Liverpudlian accent sounds a bit American.

REPORTER: When are you going to retire?

RINGO: We're going to keep going as long as we can.

GEORGE: When we get fed up with it. We're still enjoying it now, and as long as we enjoy it, we'll do it, because we enjoyed it before we made any money.

REPORTER: What do you think of Beethoven?

RINGO: Great! Especially his poems. [He laughs.]

David Pritchard and Alan Lysaght, *The Beatles: An Oral History.* New York: Hyperion, 1998.

DOCUMENT 5: SELF-DEPRECATING WIT DOWN UNDER

On June 12, 1964, the Beatles gave a press conference in Adelaide, Australia. Their wit was up to its usual standard, but John's responses were more humbling—showing some of his dissatisfaction with the hype that surrounded the band.

QUESTION: Paul, what do you expect to find here in Australia?

JOHN: Australians, I should think.

QUESTION: Do you have an acknowledged leader of the group?

JOHN: No, not really.

QUESTION: We heard that you stood on your head on the balcony outside, is that right?

PAUL: I don't know where you hear these rumors.

QUESTION: John, has the Mersey Beat changed much since you've been playing it?

JOHN: There's no such thing as Mersey Beat. The press made that up. It's all rock'n'roll.

QUESTION: Do you play the same way now as you did?

JOHN: It's only rock'n'roll. It just so happens that we write most of it.

QUESTION: Did Buddy Holly influence your music?

JOHN: He did in the early days. Obviously he was one of the greats.

PAUL: So did James Thurber, though, didn't he?

JOHN: Yeah, but he doesn't sing as well, does he?

QUESTION: Have you been practicing up your Australian accents?

GEORGE: No, guvnor, not at all.

QUESTION: Do you think you will be writing any songs with Australian themes?

JOHN: No, we never write anything with themes. We just write the same rubbish all the time.

Geoffrey Giuliano, *The Lost Beatles Interviews.* New York: Dutton, 1994.

DOCUMENT 6: THE HAZARDS OF FAME

Brian Epstein, the Beatles' manager, recalls an unsettling incident at a reception in Adelaide, Australia, in which Ringo's hair was criticized and nearly grabbed by another guest. This and other threatening episodes were simply the dark side of Beatlemania, according to Epstein.

At an elegant civic reception in Adelaide, autograph pencils flashed like knives around the valuable features of Lennon, Harrison, and McCartney and it was a relief when the Lord Mayor of Melbourne barred autographs at his reception in honor of the Beatles. There, too, was one tricky incident when a young man made an offensive remark about the length of Ringo's hair, repeated it, and then lunged forward to grab it.

He was jabbed smartly in the ribs by the sharp elbow of an otherwise nonviolent Beatle-minder and later complained, with surprising naïveté that he had been attacked.

Ringo's hair is an occupational hazard. For at the sprawling, appalling British Embassy reception in Washington there was the incident of the scissors when a guest snipped off a curl of the famous locks.

Is it surprising that we take a long hard look at receptions at embassies?

The Beatles run other risks. The more obvious ones are on stage in the worldwide barrage of jelly-beans, pennies, toys, autograph books, and, indeed, anything throwable.

Paul was nearly blinded once by a safety-pin, George took a sharp knock in Hong Kong when a silver dollar struck him on the ear. Thus are the many demonstrations of love manifested violently. . . .

It is not all danger, however, and I find all large gatherings of fans immensely exhilarating and thrilling. I can think of no warmer experience than to be in a vast audience at a Beatle concert.

I hope Beatle crowds continue to scream themselves hoarse in a frenzy of exultation.

I hope everybody has a wildly, wonderfully, good time. For this—and only this—is what the Beatles are all about.

Brian Epstein, *A Cellarful of Noise: The Autobiography of the Man Who Made the Beatles.* New York: Byron Preiss, 1998.

DOCUMENT 7: WHERE DOES THE MONEY GO?

In May 1965, George Harrison responded to questions from the UK press. In one answer, George reveals his concern over his bandmates' lack of interest in where their considerable fortunes are being spent or invested.

I'm not really the most interested in money Beatle, I'm just the only one interested in what's happening to it. I like to know where it's going. Actually I can't quite understand why the others aren't so bothered. We sit at accountants meetings and we are told we have got two and a half per cent of this and four and a half per cent of that, and that is confusing and boring and just like being back at school. Well, after a year or so of the Beatles making records and doing well, I started trying to find out what was happening and where it was going. John and Paul were equally interested, but they gave in. I didn't. It's easy to get blasé and think we're making plenty and somebody's taking care of it. But I like to know how much is coming in; where it's being put; and how much I spend. We all have some private investments. Believe it or not, we still haven't got a terrific amount of money in real capital. There are a lot of group investments in the name of Beatles Ltd. obviously because that's a very safe thing. There are lump sums in bank deposit accounts in the names of all four of us, I believe. There isn't a million pounds in cash or anything like that. It's mostly investments. Ringo has got his brick-building company and John and I have got a supermarket somewhere, but I don't know where it is exactly. I don't know about Paul. I'm sure that he has got some good investments as well.

Keith Badman, *The Beatles Off the Record: Outrageous Opinions and Unrehearsed Interviews.* London: Omnibus Press, 2000.

DOCUMENT 8: MORE POPULAR THAN JESUS

In a 1966 interview with journalist Maureen Cleave, John Lennon suggested that the Beatles were more popular than Jesus Christ. Although both Cleave and Lennon later explained that John was talking about his belief in the decline of Christianity's power in the modern world—and not boasting of the Beatles' fame, many Christians took offense. In America's Bible Belt, the reaction was immediate as many religious leaders and disc jockeys staged rallies in which Beatles records were burned.

Christianity will go. It will vanish and shrink. I needn't argue about that; I'm right and will be proved right. We're more popular than Jesus now; I don't know which will go first, rock'n'roll or Christianity. Jesus was all right, but his disciples were thick and ordinary. It's them twisting it that ruins it for me.

Geoffrey Giuliano, *The Lost Beatles Interviews.* New York: Dutton, 1994.

DOCUMENT 9: JOHN'S APOLOGY

To redress the backlash generated by his controversial statement about Jesus, John Lennon held a press conference in which he argued that his words were taken out of context. He defended his own beliefs and maintained that he was not "anti-God, anti-Christ, or antireligion."

JOHN: Look, I wasn't saying the Beatles are better than God or Jesus. I said "Beatles" because it's easy for me to talk about Beatles. I could have said TV or the cinema, motor cars or anything popular and I would have gotten away with it. My views on Christianity are directly influenced by *The Passover Plot* by Hugh J. Schonfield. The premise is that Jesus' message had been garbled by his disciples and twisted for a variety of self-serving reasons by those who followed, to the point where it has lost validity for many in the modern age. The passage which caused all the trouble was part of a long profile Maureen Cleave was doing for the *London Evening Standard.* Then, the mere fact that it was in *Datebook* [magazine] changed its meaning that much more.

QUESTION: What was your own formal religious background?

JOHN: Normal Church of England, Sunday School and church. But there was actually nothing going on in the church I went to. Nothing really touched us.

QUESTION: How about when you got older?

JOHN: By the time I was nineteen, I was cynical about religion and never even considered the goings-on in Christianity. It's only in the last two years that I, all the Beatles, have started looking for something else. We live in a moving hothouse. We've been mushroom-grown, forced to grow up a bit quick, like having thirty- to forty-year-old heads in twenty-year-old bodies. We had to develop more sides, more attitudes. If you're a bus man, you usually have a bus man's attitude. But we had to be more than four mopheads up there on stage. We had to grow up or we'd have been swamped.

QUESTION: Just what were you trying to get across with your comments then, sir?

JOHN: I'm not anti-God, anti-Christ, or antireligion. I was not saying we are greater or better.

QUESTION: Mr. Lennon, do you believe in God?

JOHN: I believe in God, but not as one thing, not as an old man in the sky. I believe that what people call God is something in all of us. I believe that what Jesus, Mohammed, Buddha, and all the rest said was right. It's just that the translations have gone wrong.

QUESTION: Are you sorry about your statement concerning Christ?

JOHN: I wasn't saying whatever they're saying I was saying. I'm sorry I said it, really. I never meant it to be a lousy antireligious thing. From what I've read, or observed, Christianity just seems to me to be shrinking, to be losing contact.

QUESTION: Why did you subject yourself to a public apology in front of television cameras?

JOHN: If I were at the stage I was five years ago, I would have shouted we'd never tour again, packed myself off, and that would be the end of it. Lord knows, I don't need the money. But the record burning, that was a real shock, the physical burning. I couldn't go away knowing that I'd created another little pocket of hate in the world. Especially with something as uncomplicated as people listening to records, dancing, and enjoying what the Beatles are. Not when I could do something about it. If I said tomorrow I'm not going to play again, I still couldn't live with somebody hating me for something so irrational.

Geoffrey Giuliano, *The Lost Beatles Interviews*. New York: Dutton, 1994.

DOCUMENT 10: METAMORPHOSIS

The Beatles talk about how they fit in with the counterculture of 1966 and 1967, especially the hippie scene in America.

RINGO: Growing moustaches was just part of being a hippy: you grow your hair, you grow a moustache, and in my case you grow a beard. That was the Sixties coming to the fore.

I always hated shaving anyway, but the moustache was not special for me. The moustache was growing and the beard was growing—hair was growing. It was just part of the set. We were gradually turning into Sgt Peppers. It was as if we were going through a metamorphosis. . . .

JOHN: That bit about "we changed everybody's hairstyles"—something influenced us, whatever was in the air. Pinpointing who did what first doesn't work. We were part of whatever the Sixties was. It was happening itself. *We* were the ones chosen to represent what was going on "on the street." It could have been somebody else but it wasn't: it was us and the [Rolling] Stones and people like that.

RINGO: The Beatles were *the* influence on other bands in 1966/67. It is interesting that when we got to LA and relaxed more and started hanging out with people like David Crosby, Jim Keltner, Jim McGuinn, we realised how much people were trying to be like us. Not those *particular* people, but they were telling us about other bands. We heard that producers were telling everyone to sound like the Beatles.

GEORGE: I came back to England towards the end of October and John got back from Spain. It was all predetermined when we'd meet again. Then we went in the studio and recorded "Strawberry Fields". I think at that point there was a more profound ambience to the band.

The Beatles, *The Beatles Anthology*. San Francisco: Chronicle, 2000.

DOCUMENT 11: FALLING IN LOVE WITH *SGT. PEPPER'S*

EMI producer George Martin relates his feelings upon hearing the early version of "Strawberry Fields Forever," John Lennon's dreamy composition that became a focal point of Sgt. Pepper's Lonely Hearts Club Band.

It is impossible for me to talk about *Sgt. Pepper* without mentioning two crucial songs that neatly bracket it: 'Strawberry Fields Forever' and 'All You Need Is Love'. If 'All You Need Is Love' says everything about where the Beatles were in terms of popularity and success, 'Strawberry Fields Forever' shows us where they were musically. Destined originally to be on *Pepper*, it set the agenda for the whole album.

I am not sure how much cold-blooded analysis has to do with one's passion for a work of art. It is a bit like falling in love. Do we really care if there is the odd wrinkle here or there? The power to move people, to tears or laughter, to violence or sympathy, is the strongest attribute that any art can have. In this respect, music is the prime mover: its call on the emotions is the most direct of all the arts.

An initial gut reaction to a piece of music is almost always right. When I first heard 'Strawberry Fields Forever', I was thrilled. When I hear it now, it can still send a shiver along my spine.

I heard it first on a cold windy night in November 1966. We were in Abbey Road's Studio No. 2. John was standing in front of me, his acoustic guitar at the ready. This was his usual way of showing me a new song—another of my extremely privileged private performances . . . 'It's goes something like this, George,' he said, with a nonchalance that concealed his ingrained diffidence about his voice. Then he began strumming gently.

A couple of introductory chords, and we were straight into that starry, echoing line: 'Living is easy with eyes closed. . . .' That wonderfully distinctive voice had a slight tremor, a unique nasal quality that gave his song poignancy, almost a feeling of lumine scence. I was spellbound. I was in love.

George Martin, with William Pearson, *With a Little Help from My Friends: The Making of Sgt. Pepper.* New York: Little, Brown, 1994.

DOCUMENT 12: PAST MISTAKES, NEW VENTURES

In a press conference in New York in 1968, John Lennon and Paul McCartney answer questions about breaking with the Maharishi Mahesh Yogi and beginning their new business called Apple.

QUESTION: Why did you leave the Maharishi?

JOHN: We made a mistake.

QUESTION: Do you think other people are making a mistake as well?

JOHN: That's up to them. We're human.

QUESTION: What do you mean, you made a mistake?

JOHN: That's all, you know.

PAUL: We thought there was more to him than there was, but he's human and for a while we thought he wasn't.

QUESTION: Could you tell us about your newest corporate business venture [Apple]?

JOHN: It's a business concerning records, films, and electronics and, as a sideline, manufacturing or whatever. We want to set up a system whereby people who just want to make a film about anything don't have to go on their knees in somebody's office, probably yours.

PAUL: We really want to help people, but without doing it like charity or seeming like ordinary patrons of the arts. I mean, we're in the happy position of not really needing any more money, so for the first time the bosses aren't in it for the profit. If you come to see me and say, "I've had such and such a dream," I will say, "Here's so much money. Go away and do it." We've already bought all our dreams, so now we want to share that possibility with others. There's no desire in any of our heads to take over the world. That was Hitler. There, is, however, a desire to get power in order to use it for the good.

JOHN: The aim of this company isn't really a stack of gold teeth in bank. We've done that bit. It's more of a trick to see if we can actually get artistic freedom within a business structure, to see if we can create nice things and sell them without charging three times our cost.

QUESTION: How will you run your new company?

JOHN: There's people we can get to do that. We don't know anything about business.

Geoffrey Giuliano, *The Lost Beatles Interviews.* New York: Dutton, 1994.

DOCUMENT 13: I THOUGHT IT WAS YOU THREE!

During the recording of the Beatles' White Album (The Beatles), *the band rarely worked as a unit. Ringo Starr, who was not in on the composing of the music, felt detached from the band and believed his drumming was not up to par. Feeling morose, Ringo walked out of the band for a short time. Later Ringo recalled the shaky relations and general unease all the Beatles experienced during the White Album sessions.*

While we were recording the 'White' album we ended up being more of a band again, and that's what I always love. I love being in a band. Of course, I must have had moments of turmoil, because I left the group for a while that summer.

I left because I felt two things: I felt I wasn't playing great, and I also felt that the other three were really happy and I was an outsider. I went to see John, who had been living in my apartment in Montagu Square with Yoko since he moved out of Kenwood. I said,

'I'm leaving the group because I'm not playing well and I feel unloved and out of it, and you three are really close. And John said, 'I thought it was *you three!*'

So then I went over to Paul's and knocked on his door. I said the same thing: 'I'm leaving the band. I feel you three guys are really close and I'm out of it.' And Paul said, 'I thought it was *you three!* '

I didn't even bother going to George then. I said, 'I'm going on holiday.' I took the kids and we went to Sardinia.

The Beatles, *The Beatles Anthology.* San Francisco: Chronicle, 2000.

DOCUMENT 14: UNDER THE SHADOW OF LENNON-MCCARTNEY

In July 1969, George Harrison admits that, as a songwriter, he has always felt intimidated by the more prolific Lennon-McCartney team. With a growing confidence in his own work, however, George reveals his aim of getting more of his music recorded.

I've got about forty tunes which I haven't recorded, and some of them I think are quite good. I wrote one called 'The Art Of Dying' three years ago, and at that time I thought it was too far out. But I'm going to record it. I used to have a hang-up about telling John, Paul and Ringo I had a song for the albums, because I felt mentally, at that time, as if I was trying to compete. And, in a way, the standard of the songs had to be good, because theirs were very good. Another thing is I didn't want the Beatles to be recording rubbish for my sake, just because I wrote it. On the other hand, I don't want to record rubbish just because they wrote it. The group comes first. It took time for me to get more confidence as a songwriter, and now I don't care if they don't like it. I can shrug it off. Another thing with the Beatles is it's sometimes a matter of whoever pushes the hardest gets the most tunes on the album, then it's down to personalities, as to whoever is going to push. And more often, I just leave it until somebody says that they would like to do one of my tunes.

Keith Badman, *The Beatles Off the Record: Outrageous Opinions and Unrehearsed Interviews.* London: Omnibus Press, 2000.

DOCUMENT 15: NO SOLUTION BUT PEACE

In an interview in London in late 1969, John Lennon maintains that peaceful demonstrations are the only means of defeating the "establishment," the force in power that is responsible for much of the violence in the world. Although he sticks by this philosophy, John admits that he does not have the answers to the problems of the times.

Some people discovered a new reality and are still confident about the future, like the two of us. Everyone's talking about the way its going, the decadence and the rest of it, but hardly anyone's talking about all the good that came out of the last ten years. Like the vast gathering of people at Woodstock, which was the biggest mass of people ever gathered together for anything other than war. Before, nobody had an army that big that wasn't there to kill somebody or have a violent scene like the Romans. Even a Beatle concert was more violent than that! The good things to come out of the last ten years were these peaceful movements. The bully, that's the establishment. They know how to beat people up, they know how to gas them. They have the arms and the equipment. The mistake was made when the kids started playing their game. Nobody can tell me that violence is the way. There *must* be another way. But a lot of people fell for it, and it's actually understandable, because when the bully is actually right there it's hard to say, "Turn the other cheek, baby!" When we were in touch with the kids in Berkeley [who were battling the University of California over developing People's Park in May 1969], we were doing our peace demonstration in Montreal in bed and we were suddenly directly connected to them by phone. They were saying, "Help us! It's out of our control." What can we say? I haven't got any solution!

Geoffrey and Vrnda Giuliano, *Things We Said Today: Conversations with the Beatles.* Holbrook, MA: Adams Media, 1998.

DOCUMENT 16: ANSWERING THE INEVITABLE QUESTION

In an interview with Daily Mirror *journalist Don Short on March 7, 1970, George Harrison tries to answer the oft-repeated question, "Have the Beatles split up for all time?"*

Everybody keeps asking the same question. There are some people around who can't imagine the world without the Beatles. That's what it must be. But this had to happen. We had to find ourselves, individually, one day. It was the natural course of events. The thing is that people think we know all the answers about the Beatles and we don't. Who are we? We can't give the answer, and I, for one, can't define that special something else that made us as we are. It wasn't just the records, or our concerts. You tell me. We've all left the Beatles one by one. I left because of a musical policy dispute with Paul; Ringo went into films; and John got into the bed-in bit with Yoko; and now Paul's making his own album. It's true we don't see much of Paul, but he's gone off the 'coming-into-the-office' scene. He wants to be quiet and left alone and he doesn't want to create any ripples. And after ten years, he deserves to be quiet. I'm going to disappear soon myself for a rest. I'll probably go back to India for a while. Yes, maybe when this year's over and we've got out of all the things we're into, we will get back. We just can't stop being Beatles whatever we do. Besides, we're contracted to each other until 1977. Funny, I didn't discover that myself until the other day. I don't think the others know yet. But it's all unity through diversity, Don. That's why I dig the title 'Let It Be' just now, because it fits the picture. Why try and fight the natural turn of events?

Keith Badman, *The Beatles Off the Record: Outrageous Opinions and Unrehearsed Interviews.* London: Omnibus Press, 2000.

DOCUMENT 17: WE'RE STILL LIKE BROTHERS

During a 1970 interview in London just prior to quitting the Beatles, Paul McCartney insisted that he was not responsible for dissolving the band. Although he maintained that George and Ringo had each walked out on the Beatles in the past year, it was John who first decided that his relationship with Yoko Ono would require a "divorce" from the band.

The real breakup of the Beatles was months ago. Ringo left when we were doing the White album, because he said it wasn't fun playing with us anymore. But after two days of us telling him he was the greatest drummer in the world for the Beatles, which I believe, he came back. Then George left when we were making *Abbey Road* because he said he didn't think he had enough say on our records, which was fair enough. After a couple of days he came back. Then last autumn I began to feel the only way we could ever get back to playing good music was to start behaving as a band. But I didn't want to go out and face 200,000 people because I would get nothing from it, so I thought up this idea of playing surprise one-night stands in unlikely places. So one day when we had a meeting and I told the others about my idea, and asked them what they thought of it, John said, "I think you're daft!" I said, "What do you mean?" I mean he is John Lennon, and I'm a bit scared of all that rapier wit we hear about. And he just said, "I think you're daft. I'm leaving the Beatles. I want a divorce." John's in love with Yoko, and he's no longer in love with the three of us. Let's face it, we were in love with the Beatles as much as anyone. We're still like brothers.

Geoffrey and Vrnda Giuliano, *Things We Said Today: Conversations with the Beatles.* Holbrook, MA: Adams Media, 1998.

DISCUSSION QUESTIONS

1. How were the Beatles (or their early incarnations) similar to other bands in England in the late 1950s and early 1960s? How were they different? Examine such elements as music styles, musical influences, appearance, and stage presence when answering these questions.

2. What aspects of the band that were molded during the early tours of England and Germany remained part of the Beatles' character in later years? What aspects noticeably changed?

CHAPTER 2

1. Hunter Davies describes Beatlemania in England as "a phenomenon of mass communication." What does he mean? What elements had to be in place for this phenomenon to occur?

2. In what ways was Beatlemania in England similar to Beatlemania in America? In what ways was it different? In answering, be sure to examine how English society in the 1960s compared to American society.

3. Hunter Davies acknowledges that there were many critics of the Beatles and Beatlemania in Britain and America during the 1960s. Reread some of these criticisms and discuss their validity. Why do you think these critics chose the Beatles as a target? There are similar backlashes against pop celebrities today, but are modern criticisms any different than the condemnations leveled against the Beatles? Explain.

CHAPTER 3

1. According to Bob Neaverson, how did the Beatles' films support their changing image? What impact did the first three movies have on American and British film and television at the time? Watch *A Hard Day's Night* and decide if there are any movies in more recent times that seem to

incorporate either the theme or style of Richard Lester's movie.

2. Looking at the claims made by Allan F. Moore, how were the Beatles musically influenced by the psychedelic scene in the late 1960s? Listen to some of the tracks on *Revolver* and *Sgt. Pepper's Lonely Hearts Club Band* and explain how the music and lyrics could be said to reflect psychedelic experiences.

3. What do you think the Beatles (especially John Lennon and George Harrison) were looking for when they became disciples of the Maharishi Mahesh Yogi? Do you think the Beatles would have followed the maharishi if they had met him in 1962? What was it about the Beatles' careers in 1966 that might have influenced or facilitated their decision to investigate Indian mysticism?

CHAPTER 4

1. After reading the articles in this chapter, explain what factors led to the breakup of the Beatles. Do you think any one factor stands out as the most influential? Explain why.

2. Follow up some of the "Paul is dead" rumors to weigh the evidence for yourself. Do you think Paul McCartney died in 1966? Why do you think people were (and to some extent still are) willing to believe in Paul's untimely death? In answering, think of what other events of the 1960s were compounded by rumors and uncorroborated conjecture.

CHAPTER 5

1. Both Charles Paul Freund and Kevin Michael Grace offer explanations for the Beatles' enduring popularity. Do you think one or the other (or both) capture the essence of why the Beatles are still liked or revered by generations born after the band's demise? What other explanations might you offer to explain why the Beatles are still popular?

2. Consider the different periods of Beatles' music and songwriting. Which period or periods do you like the best? Explain which types of Beatles' songs you like the least and why.

CHRONOLOGY

OCTOBER 18, 1957

In Liverpool, England, Paul McCartney plays his first show with John Lennon and the rest of his band, the Quarry Men.

FEBRUARY 6, 1958

Paul introduces his schoolmate, fourteen-year-old George Harrison, to the Quarry Men; Harrison joins the band and plays his first show in March.

JANUARY 1960

John's art-college friend Stuart Sutcliffe joins the Quarry Men to play bass guitar; the band receives no bookings through March, but in March, they change their name to the Beatals in honor of the Crickets, Buddy Holly's band.

MAY 1960

The band, rechristened the Silver Beetles, tours Scotland in support of Johnny Gentle.

AUGUST 12, 1960

Pete Best joins the slightly renamed Silver Beatles; in four days, the band sets off to play in Hamburg, Germany; they perform in Hamburg clubs simply as the Beatles.

DECEMBER 1960

After several mishaps, including George Harrison's deportation, most of the band ends up back in England; Stuart Sutcliffe, however, remains in Hamburg to get engaged to photographer Astrid Kirchherr and return to art school.

FEBRUARY 9, 1961

The four remaining Beatles debut at the Cavern Club in Liverpool.

APRIL 1, 1961

The Beatles return to the clubs in Hamburg (and even play a few shows with Stuart Sutcliffe).

JUNE 22–23, 1961

Probably on these dates, the Beatles record in a Hamburg studio (under the name the Beat Brothers) as a backing band for singer Tony Sheridan; they return to Liverpool soon after.

DECEMBER 3, 1961

Record store manager Brian Epstein offers to manage the Beatles; the band accepts three days later.

FEBRUARY 13, 1962

After failing to impress Decca Records, Epstein has the Beatles audition for Parlophone A&R man George Martin.

APRIL 10, 1962

As the band returns to Hamburg for another tour, they are met at the plane by Astrid Kirchherr; she tells them that Stuart Sutcliffe died earlier that day of cerebral paralysis.

JUNE 4, 1962

Back in Liverpool, the band signs a recording contract with EMI, Parlophone's parent corporation; two days later they make their first major-label recordings.

AUGUST 16, 1962

Epstein fires Pete Best, ostensibly at the other band members' request; two days later, Ringo Starr (former drummer of Rory and the Hurricanes) joins the Beatles.

OCTOBER 5, 1962

"Love Me Do" single is released in England.

FEBRUARY 25, 1963

"Please Please Me" is the first Beatles' single released in the United States.

OCTOBER 13, 1963

The Beatles play the London Palladium, a televised performance that is watched by 15 million British viewers; the show marks the beginning of Beatlemania in the UK.

DECEMBER 4, 1963

The Beatles play a Royal Command Performance at Prince of Wales Theatre in London.

FEBRUARY 7, 1964

The Beatles arrive at Kennedy Airport in New York to begin their U.S. tour.

FEBRUARY 9, 1964

The Beatles appear on *The Ed Sullivan Show;* an estimated 73 million viewers tune in to watch the performance.

MARCH 21, 1964

"She Loves You" single tops the U.S. charts.

JUNE 4, 1964

The Beatles begin their tour of the Far East; Ringo Starr is sick and replaced for the initial tour dates.

JULY 6, 1964

Richard Lester's film *A Hard Day's Night* premieres in London.

AUGUST 15, 1964

On their second American tour, the Beatles play to a crowd of over fifty-five thousand at Shea Stadium.

SEPTEMBER 26, 1964

The Beatles are made members of the Order of the British Empire at Buckingham Palace; John Lennon will later renounce his award and return his medal in 1969.

AUGUST 29, 1966

The Beatles perform at Candlestick Park in San Francisco; they announce an end to touring; within a short time, rumors suggest the Beatles have broken up.

JUNE 1, 1967

Sgt. Pepper's Lonely Hearts Club Band is released in the UK.

JUNE 16, 1967

Paul McCartney publicly admits to experimenting with LSD.

AUGUST 27, 1967

Brian Epstein is found dead from an overdose of tranquilizers.

FEBRUARY 15–19, 1968

The Beatles and their wives fly to a spiritual retreat in India with the Maharishi Mahesh Yogi.

MAY 15, 1968

On a prerecorded episode of *The Tonight Show* in America, John Lennon and Paul McCartney announce the formation of Apple Corps, the Beatles' business venture.

MAY 30, 1968

John Lennon's new girlfriend, Yoko Ono, joins the Beatles for the recording sessions of the White Album.

JULY 17, 1968

The animated film *Yellow Submarine* opens in London; the Beatles provide a soundtrack but do not lend their voices to the animated versions of themselves on-screen.

AUGUST 22, 1968

Cynthia Lennon, John's wife, sues him for divorce.

DECEMBER 18, 1968

John Lennon and Yoko Ono writhe inside a large white sack as part of a visual performance at the Royal Albert Hall.

JANUARY 30, 1969

The Beatles perform a spontaneous concert on the roof of Apple offices in London.

MARCH 25–31, 1969

After marrying, John Lennon and Yoko Ono stage a "bed-in for peace" honeymoon at the Amsterdam Hilton.

MAY 8, 1969

American businessman Allan Klein becomes the de facto manager of the Beatles' business affairs.

OCTOBER 12, 1969

Detroit disc jockey Russ Gibb helps spread a rumor that Paul McCartney died in 1966.

APRIL 10, 1970

Paul McCartney announces he is leaving the Beatles.

MAY 8, 1970

The Beatles' final album, *Let It Be*, is released in the UK.

FOR FURTHER RESEARCH

Keith Badman, *The Beatles Off the Record: Outrageous Opinions and Unrehearsed Interviews.* London: Omnibus Press, 2000.

Glenn A. Baker, *The Beatles Down Under: The 1964 Australian and New Zealand Tour.* Buckinghamshire, UK: Magnum Imprint, 1996.

The Beatles, *The Beatles Anthology.* San Francisco: Chronicle, 2000.

Pete Best and Patrick Doncaster, *Beatle!: The Pete Best Story.* London: Plexus, 2001.

Hunter Davies, *The Beatles.* 2nd rev. ed. New York: W.W. Norton, 1996.

Richard Dilello, *The Longest Cocktail Party: An Insider's Diary of the Beatles, Their Million Dollar "Apple" Empire, and Its Wild Rise and Fall.* Edinburgh, UK: MOJO Books, 2001.

Brian Epstein, *A Cellarful of Noise: The Autobiography of the Man Who Made the Beatles.* New York: Byron Preiss, 1998.

Walter Everett, *The Beatles as Musicians.* 2 vols. New York: Oxford University Press, 1999, 2001.

Charles Paul Freund, "Still Fab: The Beatles and Their Timeless Influence," *Reason,* June 2001.

Geoffrey Giuliano, *The Lost Beatles Interviews.* New York: Dutton, 1994.

Geoffrey and Vrnda Giuliano, *Things We Said Today: Conversations with the Beatles.* Holbrook, MA: Adams Media, 1998.

Kevin Michael Grace, "Beatles Forever: The Fab Four Have Gone from Pop Sensation to Cultural Artifact," *Report,* January 1, 2001.

Stefan Granados, *Those Were the Days: An Unofficial History of the Beatles' Apple Organization, 1967–2002*. London: Cherry Red Books, 2002.

Mark Hertsgaard, *A Day in the Life: The Music and Artistry of the Beatles*. New York: Delta, 1995.

Ian Inglis, ed., *The Beatles, Popular Music, and Society: A Thousand Voices*. London: Macmillan, 2000.

Paul R. Kohl, "A Splendid Time Is Guaranteed for All: The Beatles as Agents of Carnival," *Popular Music and Society*, Winter 1996.

Mark Lewisohn, *The Complete Beatles Chronicle*. New York: Harmony, 1992.

Ian MacDonald, *Revolution in the Head: The Beatles' Records and the Sixties*. New York: Henry Holt, 1994.

George Martin, with William Pearson, *With a Little Help from My Friends: The Making of Sgt. Pepper*. New York: Little, Brown, 1994.

Peter McCabe and Robert D. Schonfeld, *Apple to the Core: The Unmaking of the Beatles*. New York: Pocket Books, 1976.

Devin McKinney, *Magic Circles: The Beatles in Dream and History*. Cambridge, MA: Harvard University Press, 2003.

Allan F. Moore, *The Beatles: Sgt. Pepper's Lonely Hearts Club Band*. Cambridge, UK: Cambridge University Press, 1997.

Philip Norman, *Shout!: The Beatles in Their Generation*. New York: MJF, 1981.

Gareth L. Pawlowski, *How They Became the Beatles: A Definitive History of the Early Years, 1960–1964*. New York: E.P. Dutton, 1989.

David Pritchard and Alan Lysaght, *The Beatles: An Oral History*. New York: Hyperion, 1998.

David Quantick, *Revolution: The Making of the Beatles' White Album*. Chicago: A Cappella Books, 2002.

Russell Reising, ed., *"Every Sound There Is": The Beatles' Revolver and the Transformation of Rock and Roll*. Burlington, VT: Ashgate, 2002.

David Rowley, *Beatles for Sale: The Musical Secrets of the*

Greatest Rock 'n' Roll Band of All Time. London: Mainstream, 2002.

Nicholas Schaffner, *The Beatles Forever*. Harrisburg, PA: Cameron House, 1978.

Bruce Spizer, *The Beatles on Apple Records*. New Orleans: 498 Productions, 2003.

———, *The Beatles on Vee-Jay Records*. New Orleans: 498 Productions, 1998.

———, *The Beatles' Story on Capitol Records*. 2 vols. New Orleans: 498 Productions, 2000.

Doug Sulpy and Ray Schweighardt, *Get Back: The Unauthorized Chronicle of the Beatles' "Let It Be" Disaster*. New York: St. Martin's, 1997.

Alistair Taylor, *With the Beatles*. London: John Blake, 2003.

WEB SITES

The Beatles Ultimate Experience, www.geocities.com/~beatleboy1/db.menu.html. A privately run Web site that offers an array of Beatle interviews. Also included are pages on the Beatles' movies, their songs, and photos of the band. There is also a Beatles' trivia section.

I Am the Beatles, www.iamthebeatles.com. Among other things, this Web site features information on Beatles' songs, including lyrics, history, and meaning. The site is run by John T. Marck, a Maryland freelance writer.

The Internet Beatles Album, www.beatlesagain.com. Run by Dave Haber, this attractive Web site offers minibiographies of the Fab Four, photos, a "This Day in Beatle History" page, and a link to an archive of articles from the Internet news page rec.music.beatles.

INDEX